A GUY'S GUIDE TO
PREGNANCY
Preparing for
Parenthood Together

FRANK MUNGEAM
Foreword by John Gray, Ph.D.

MJF BOOKS
NEW YORK

The information contained in this book is intended to be educational and not for diagnosis, prescription, or treatment of mental and/or physical health disorders, whatsoever. This information should not replace competent medical and/or psychological care. The authors and publisher are in no way liable for any use or misuse of the information.

Published by MJF Books
Fine Communications
Two Lincoln Square
60 West 66th Street
New York, NY 10023

Guy's Guide to Pregnancy
Library of Congress Catalog Card Number 98-68234
ISBN 1-56731-314-0

This edition published by arrangement with Beyond Words Publishing, Inc.

Design: Principia Graphica

Manufactured in the United States of America on acid-free paper

MJF Books and the MJF colophon are trademarks of Fine Creative Media, Inc.

10   9   8   7   6   5   4   3   2   1

CONTENTS

FOREWORD

As I read through *A Guy's Guide to Pregnancy*, I was reminded of the time when my wife, Bonnie, was pregnant with our daughter. In my eyes she looked especially beautiful and radiant. The whole experience taught me valuable insights about listening, love, vulnerability, and responsibility—especially the responsibility we face when we bring another life into this world. It also reminded me of how a pregnancy can magnify the differences and difficulties between men and women.

In my book *Men Are from Mars, Women Are from Venus*, I talk about how essential it is to ask for the love and support you need in a relationship. This is *especially* true when a woman is pregnant. Communication and sensitivity to your partner's needs will help your relationship through this challenging but rewarding time.

Until now, pregnancy hasn't come with a how-to manual or a tool kit. *A Guy's Guide to Pregnancy* will give you what you need to make it through the next nine months and still be married.

For example, this book shows you that just because your partner may not tell you that she expects your help with things around the house, it doesn't mean that everything is flowing smoothly. It probably means that she is doing a lot of the work as well as carrying your child. You can score big points by asking her daily, "What can I do for you?" And then do it.

Frank Mungeam outlines countless easy ways to let her know she is supported: go with her to the doctor's office, take a minute to write a loving note, send her cut flowers, accidentally break the scale, tell her that you love her, tell her that she is beautiful—often! These are simple but crucial steps you can take that will make a world of difference.

A Guy's Guide to Pregnancy is about more than handing out cigars and using your new video camera. It helps every guy understand the changes that are coming. This book also acknowledges the real needs that we, as men, face during these transitional months and offers tips for smoothing conflicts that may arise.

I hope *A Guy's Guide to Pregnancy* will be helpful to you as you begin your journey toward parenthood. Remember to keep your sense of humor. Pregnancy doesn't last forever, but the joy you feel and the love you will both have for this new child and each other will last a lifetime.

John Gray, author of
Men Are from Mars, Women Are from Venus

INTRODUCTION

Congratulations. You are on your way to joining a select fraternity—the few, the proud, the men who can say, "I survived my partner's pregnancy."

You might protest: "*Men* don't need a pregnancy book." On the contrary! Men may not experience morning sickness, weight gain, fatigue, cravings, hormonal changes, and wild mood swings, but we still need a *little* help. After all, our partner is . . . a pregnant woman.

Bookstores offer few answers. Most pregnancy books read like medical texts and focus on women. Guys have different needs and different questions.

A Guy's Guide to Pregnancy is written from a man's viewpoint to help you understand how pregnancy will affect you, your partner, and your relationship.

Does pregnancy mean an end to Boys' Night Out and sex? What do you say the first time she asks, "Do I look fat?" Is there anything you can do to keep from passing out in the delivery room? These are the questions that men want answered.

Unfortunately, if you open your partner's pregnancy guide, you're more likely to learn that a fetal ultrasound resonance during the first trimester is premature as a tool for fetal developmental analysis. Hmm.

Do you want to sift through her 450-page treatise? Or get just the information you need in a book by guys and for guys? I thought so.

Here's more good news. By reading this book, you will take a big step toward satisfying your partner's Mandatory Minimum Requirement for Male Participation.

Every woman carries inside her the unspoken expectation that you, as a caring partner and future parent, will take an active interest in her pregnancy. A woman interprets her partner's failure to read *her* pregnancy book as a sign of a lack of caring. By reading *A Guy's Guide to Pregnancy*, you'll make her happy *and* you will actually understand much of what is happening to her body.

I've written *A Guy's Guide to Pregnancy* so you can find out, from my own experience and that of other men, what to expect during the coming months. When it comes to the real technical details, I have included advice from actual *experts*, but mostly you'll see pregnancy through the eyes of myself and five other regular guys as we describe what it was like for us at each stage of our partners' pregnancies. Plus, you'll also get free advice from actual moms. In the back of the book are the profiles of the people behind the stories.

I've organized this book into forty brief chapters, each focusing on one of the issues you're likely to face during the next forty weeks.

You'll learn answers to the most common questions guys ask, you'll discover that many of your fears are normal concerns shared by other men, and you'll learn useful things to help you and your partner have a positive pregnancy experience.

A Guy's Guide to Pregnancy takes an intentionally lighthearted approach to this very important transition in your life. After all, your sense of humor will often be your best tool for coping with the dramatic changes happening to your partner's body and to your relationship together.

part

ONE

1 STARTING
OUT

1 MAKING BABIES

Let's talk about sex.

"Sex = fun." Right? Not necessarily. The decision to start a family can sometimes change this equation. All too often, the moment you and your partner decide to expand, the formula becomes "sex = making babies." In some cases, it eventually becomes "sex = work."

If you're lucky, you will get your partner pregnant in the first month and you'll be able to brag about your virility to all of your guy friends. Your partner will look at you with admiring eyes. Life will be good.

More likely, you'll be like normal people and need more than one night at the slot machine of conception before you finally hit the sperm-egg-embryo jackpot.

The problem is, once you and your partner decide to start a family, she'll want to be pregnant *immediately*. Unfortunately, the odds of that happening are about the same as they are in Vegas—although losing is cheaper and a lot more fun.

BY THE NUMBERS

Approximately half of the women who plan their pregnancies conceive within three and one-half months. One in five try for more than nine months before becoming pregnant.

Still, it won't be long before her initial excitement that "We're going to make a baby!" becomes the worrying question of "Am I pregnant yet?" You may begin to feel guilt and self-doubt, not to mention a little performance anxiety. Worst of all, making love may start to seem like a chore.

GUY TALK

The doctor told my wife, "It may take you up to nine months to conceive because of the stress of your work schedule, your physical activity, and so on." That was on Wednesday. On Saturday we conceived! Super swimmers!
—John

Soon, she'll be "scheduling" sex when her "cycles" are right—it's all very scientific stuff—and you will feel like the telephone repairman, coming by at specific times to do your job. When my wife and I were trying to conceive, it began to feel less like trying to start a family and more like some complex scientific experiment.

After a while, you'll wonder how *anyone* ever had an "unwanted pregnancy," since when you *want* a baby you can't seem to accomplish the feat.

You will start worrying, "Is it me?" And worse, "Will I have to go to a doctor and endure *those* tests?"

Before you panic, try to look at the bright side. If you're not getting her pregnant, you can at least have fun *trying*. Countless men would love to be in your situation—regular lovemaking without fear of conception.

One day, when you least expect it, your partner will greet you and break the big news: She's pregnant!

② "YOU'RE GOING TO BE A DAD!"

You'll never forget the moment your partner tells you she's pregnant—probably because she'll do it right in the middle of the big game!

Everyone reacts differently to this news. You might cry tears of joy, or you might respond with shocked surprise, even though you had quite a bit to do with making this happen.

For most guys, this is the first time we realize the magnitude of what we've done. Panic may set in. Parenthood is no longer some theoretical possibility. You're going to be a dad!

You may have jumbled visions of dirty diapers, potty training, Little League games, curfew arguments, report cards, first dates, and wrecked cars.

You might also want a stiff drink. I don't blame you. This is a big deal. Expect to be afraid.

The top ten fears of expectant dads
1. My partner will turn into a crazy woman.
2. My partner will get fat and unattractive.
3. She'll never lose her pregnancy weight gain.
4. We'll never have any money again.
5. I'll never see my guy friends again.
6. I'll never be able to have sex with my partner again after seeing the delivery.
7. I'll have to deliver the baby.
8. I'll faint during the delivery.
9. We won't have a healthy baby.
10. I'm not ready—I won't be a good dad.

Some of these fears are well-founded. Fortunately, many are not. Here's the good news and the bad news:

GUY TALK

I found out on my birthday. I came home with a six-pack of beer . . . and she handed me a birthday card and said here you go . . . and the card said something like "Happy Birthday— I know you'll be a great father"!
—Michael

My partner will turn into a crazy woman

True. Fortunately, you'll get her back. You'll just have to wait nine months. For help, see chapter 3.

My partner will get fat and unattractive

Yes and no. She will gain plenty of weight, but many men are delighted to discover how beautiful their partners look to them during pregnancy. If you're one of those men who isn't delighted, don't worry. Pregnancy is temporary. Unless you're also afraid that . . .

She'll never lose her pregnancy weight gain

Most women lose most of their pregnancy weight. However, let's give them a break if their bodies change slightly as a result of bearing our child. After all, they are going to carry a twenty-five-pound weight for nine months and then have the pleasure of spending a day pushing a very large object through a very small opening.

We'll never have any money again

True! Children are a financial black hole. The average household spends nearly $10,000 in the first year on their new baby.

For your sake, I hope you bought that surround sound system before you found out she was pregnant.

I'll never see my guy friends again

Probably. You'll pay so dearly every time you party with them while your poor pregnant partner stays home that you'll choose the lesser penalty and keep her company.

For tips on negotiating more Guy Time, see chapter 21.

I'll never be able to have sex with my partner again after seeing the delivery

Many guys have this concern. In reality, there's another reason why couples might not resume sex immediately after their child is born: They're so *exhausted* that all their bed-related fantasies involve sleeping.

Don't worry, you *will* still have sex after your baby is born. You'll just be darned careful about accidentally making another "junior"—because by then you'll understand the consequences.

The corollary fear is, "Does pregnancy mean no more sex for nine months?"

Not necessarily. Some women find that pregnancy increases their sexual appetite. For others the reverse is true. A lot depends on you and your creativity. For helpful hints, see chapter 12.

I'll have to deliver the baby

You have been watching too much television. The odds are you'll have your baby in the hospital like everyone else.

If you're really paranoid about this possibility, my advice would be to avoid taking a cab to the hospital, since cabs always seem to be the place where people do wind up delivering their own babies.

I'll faint during the delivery

Or the related fear, "I'll stay on my feet and see *everything*!" You probably won't faint, but every man worries about this. See chapter 34 for helpful hints on keeping upright.

Fortunately, once labor starts, most guys become far too engrossed in the delivery of their child to remember that they ever had this fear.

We won't have a healthy baby

This fear is a constant companion of pregnant couples. Fortunately, 97 out of 100 couples have healthy babies. You can increase your odds by making healthy diet and lifestyle choices.

I'm not ready—I won't be a good dad

If you didn't worry about being a good parent, *that* would be cause for concern. There is no right way and there is no class that can fully prepare you. Being a good dad is like being a good husband. You try to do the best you can and learn as you go. The fact that you worry about it is the best predictor that you care enough to do a good job.

She's Going to Be a Mom!

When your own shock and elation from this announcement subside, prepare for some instant changes in your partner, too.

Like you, she is reeling from the impact of this news. She'll share your combination of disbelief, terror, and joy. She'll also start to think, talk, and act like a woman possessed.

I was in a state of shock. I was dazed and confused. I swear it wasn't until about six hours later, on the freeway driving home, that it hit me. And I started crying. I was just overwhelmed with joy, and excitement, and terror!
—John

I was lying in bed suffering from the flu. My wife came into the bedroom and announced that she was pregnant. We had been trying to have a child for a while, and I knew that it was important to say something significant. All I could muster, however, was a weak "Oh, that's great." I could tell she was a little disappointed in my reaction. The impact of the news didn't fully hit me until a few hours later when my fever broke. Then I was amazed, excited, anxious, and concerned!
—Paul

I thought my wife was obsessed with details back when we were planning our wedding. Then she found out she was pregnant. All of a sudden, there were hundreds of things that had to be done *right now*—even though the baby wasn't due for over seven months!

Here are a few clues to tip you off that she's changed:

- You say a swearword (as you have for years), but this time she says, "You can't let the baby hear you talk like that."
- You buy some frivolous piece of high-tech gear (as you have for years), and she says, "We can't afford to waste money on things like that. We need to save for the baby."
- You are heading out the door to meet the guys (as usual), and she says, "Are you really going to leave me alone tonight? You know, I'm *pregnant*."

These are the early warning signs that you have entered...the Pregnancy Zone.

THE PREGNANCY ZONE

3

What you thought you knew about your relationship and your partner no longer holds true. She is growing a child inside her body and everything is about to change. You are now on a journey. . .through the Pregnancy Zone.

You will need a road map for this journey because the rules are different here. In the Pregnancy Zone, your partner's actions and words will confuse you. She'll sleep for twelve hours at a time, only to wake up and announce: "I'm tired." Or, she'll consume two helpings of a full-course meal, then complain: "I'm still hungry." Expect to be disoriented. This is one of the rules of the road in the Pregnancy Zone.

At times you may truly believe that your partner has been abducted by aliens and replaced by an imposter. In reality, she is behaving exactly the way a pregnant woman should. Unfortunately, as guys, we are not prepared for this dramatic transformation of our partner's personality and physiology.

This book will help you find your way along the twisting, turning roads at each stage in your journey through the Pregnancy Zone.

Ch-ch-changes

Your partner will experience dramatic physical and emotional changes during pregnancy. Beginning in chapter 6, I'll cover these transitions in detail. Here are the two most prominent and immediate changes you'll notice:

Physical changes
Yes, her breasts will definitely get bigger. Of course, so will her belly.

She'll be able to keep up with you at the dinner table, but you may be repulsed by her bizarre food cravings. ("How can anyone eat so much of *that*?")

There are other minor side-effects to growing a baby inside your belly, including morning sickness, fatigue, and chronic backaches.

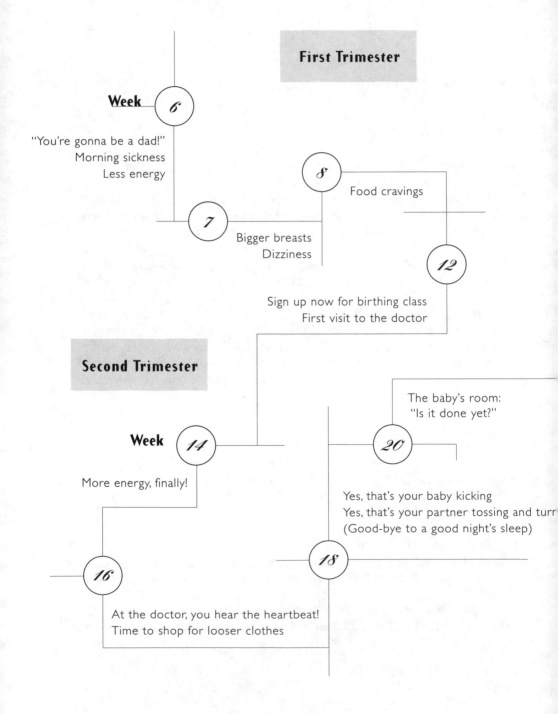

First Trimester

Week 6

"You're gonna be a dad!"
Morning sickness
Less energy

8

Food cravings

7

Bigger breasts
Dizziness

12

Sign up now for birthing class
First visit to the doctor

Second Trimester

The baby's room:
"Is it done yet?"

Week 14

20

More energy, finally!

Yes, that's your baby kicking
Yes, that's your partner tossing and turr
(Good-bye to a good night's sleep)

16

18

At the doctor, you hear the heartbeat!
Time to shop for looser clothes

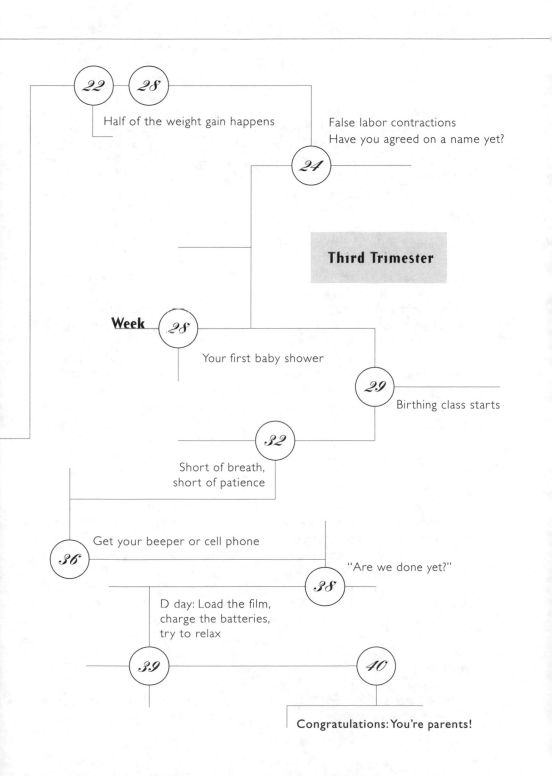

22 **23**

Half of the weight gain happens

False labor contractions
Have you agreed on a name yet?

24

Third Trimester

Week **28**

Your first baby shower

29

Birthing class starts

32

Short of breath,
short of patience

Get your beeper or cell phone

36

"Are we done yet?"

38

D day: Load the film,
charge the batteries,
try to relax

39 **40**

Congratulations: You're parents!

Personality changes

Along with the physical changes, you'll notice other differences. The moment she learns she's with baby, she'll start speaking a dialect I call "Prego Lingo" (see chapter 4). Eventually, she'll become possessed by Baby Room Frenzy (see chapter 24). You'll know because she'll insist you finish the baby's room *now*—even if "now" is four months before the baby is due.

Have you ever accused your partner of being "too emotional"? Brace yourself. Pregnancy amplifies rapid mood swings to hurricane force.

Plan on being puzzled by your partner during the coming months. Try to be patient. She will return to her usual, slightly less confusing self after the baby is born.

In the interim, there are a few things you can do to keep your sanity and support your partner.

The Golden Rule of Expectant Dads

During the next nine months, there will be moments when you are frustrated, confused, or angry. You may tire of hearing about your partner's discomforts. You might feel left out because she and the baby are getting all the attention. Toward the end, you may get fatigued because you are doing many of the tasks she did before she was pregnant.

Whenever you find yourself struggling in one of these situations, take a moment and remind yourself of the Golden Rule of Expectant Dads: "It could be worse—*you* could be pregnant."

Let's be honest. Guys have the easier half of the pregnancy experience. So whenever you catch yourself throwing a personal pity party, think of the Golden Rule of Expectant Dads. It *could* be a lot worse.

You should repeat this rule to yourself often. In addition, there's one thing you must *never* say to your partner: "I know just what you're going through."

Despite what those tabloid headlines claim, no man has ever physically experienced pregnancy, labor, or childbirth. Nor would we want to, frankly. Therefore, we would all be wise to avoid claiming we know how she feels. This is one problem that you don't need to solve and that you don't even need to fully understand.

Her body carries the baby. She's the one who has to watch what she eats, watch what she drinks, and watch her weight, stress level, and energy. She has to go to the doctor, take tests and medications, and ultimately she's the one who goes through labor and delivery.

Your Role

What's left for a guy to do? Is it time to rest up for parenthood, or are there real guy duties during these next nine months?

Based on completely unscientific conversations with frustrated moms, I can confidently declare that every pregnant woman wants two things from her partner: involvement and support.

Actually, what she wants is for *you* to be the pregnant one, for your body to balloon to 25 percent larger than normal, for you to experience labor, and for that bowling ball to pass through a small opening in your body. That's what she really wants.

Short of carrying the baby, here's the next best thing you can do for her: Participate as a partner.

You can't sub for her at the doctor's appointment, but you can go along. Your diet won't help or hurt the baby, but joining your mate in healthy eating will ease her dietary transition. You can't push during labor, but you can learn how to be her coach. You can help her in dozens of big and little ways.

Perhaps you are the type of guy who constantly reassures his partner how much he loves her and surprises her with gifts and showers her with flowers. If you are, please stop the moment your baby is born. You are making it harder for the rest of us who only do those things when reminded. But while she is pregnant we all need to rise up to the level of the over-achievers among us and make our partner feel loved. She will feel vulnerable and her body image will suffer during these nine months, so no matter how unnatural it feels to you, now is the time to be romantic and supportive. If you are out of practice, here are some suggestions:

Twelve simple things you can do to support your partner
1. Listen to her complaints without letting her know she's complaining.
2. Tell her she looks good even when you notice her weight gain.
3. Volunteer to go to the doctor's appointments with her.
4. Surprise her with flowers.
5. Skip a night out with the guys to stay home with her.
6. Resist weight jokes.
7. Pitch in more: clean the house, vacuum, do the laundry.
8. Take her on a maternity-store shopping spree.
9. Give her back and foot massages.
10. Buy her a book she likes.
11. Go to every birthing class.
12. Tell her you love her. Often.

The bottom line is that the more you can focus on trying to make her comfortable and content during these nine months, the happier you *both* will be.

To succeed, you'll need more than good intentions. You'll need a dictionary. Why? Because your wife will quickly acquire a Ph.D. in pregnancy. To keep up with her, you'll have to learn "Prego Lingo."

PREGO LINGO

Prego Lingo is not an Italian dish. It is a special language that women immediately adopt when they become pregnant.

How Long Will This Last?

Pregnancy lasts nine months, right? Wrong. Your partner knows that the correct and only acceptable answer is that pregnancy lasts "forty *weeks.*"

At first, you might think it is odd to measure such a long event in weeks. Don't worry. Nine months from now, you'll still think it's odd. Nevertheless, carrying a baby will cause your partner—and every medical professional she comes in contact with—to lose the ability to properly measure time.

After careful consideration, I've concluded that the primary purpose of measuring the pregnancy in weeks is to confuse guys. Let's face it. The math is pretty easy for the first month or so. But when you're midway through the fifth month, you could stand there for five minutes counting fingers and toes.

Of course, there are actual medical reasons for keeping track by week. Changes occur on a weekly basis, some of them predictable, and "4.25 months" doesn't really roll off the tongue. Plus, you'd have to adjust for those darned 31-day months.

So you see, the oddity of Pregnancy Time is one of those medical miracles: a creation that has the dual effect of being useful to the pregnant woman and bewildering to the guy.

If you'd like to show your partner just how thoroughly you have embraced Pregnancy Time as a unit of measurement, here are a few other events translated into their "PT" equivalent:

• Length of a football game	.02 weeks
• Recommended time between oil changes	13 weeks
• Time left to save for college	936 weeks

But Wait, There's More

Just when you've accepted weeks as the substitute measure for months, you'll be hit with the trimester curve ball. A "trimester" is one-third of the pregnancy. There is a first, middle, and last trimester (also acceptable is "first, second, and third trimesters").

If you ask a "person in the know," they'll explain that a trimester equals three months. But wait! *Months* don't exist in Prego Lingo. Trimesters should be measured in *weeks*. But forty weeks doesn't divide into three equal parts, does it? Yet nine months divides *perfectly* into three equal three-month "trimesters." Could we *possibly* have any greater proof of the Pregnancy Time conspiracy to confuse guys?

What's in a Name?

Another funny thing pregnant women do is to call the baby just plain "baby." Here's a sample sentence: "I just talked to the doctor about my ultrasound, and baby is doing fine."

You, of course, will want to run to her grammatical aid and say, "Oh, great, *the* baby is doing fine." But I guarantee she'll respond, "Yes, dear, *baby* is doing just fine."

For reasons I can't decipher, hospital people and therefore your partner will refuse to ever use *the* in relation to your baby. If it helps, just pretend you are the most unimaginative parents on the planet and you have chosen to name your baby "Baby." Baby is *the* baby's name. Just remember to change it when Baby is born.

Technical Overload

In addition to these odd behaviors, your partner will begin to hurl a continuous stream of technical terms in your general direction. Her Ph.D. in pregnancy can fuel your feelings of guy inadequacy.

Where do women learn all these terms? Pregnant women enthusiastically consume pregnancy books. This is not inherently bad. Her appetite for information will benefit her and the baby. If you had a baby growing inside *you*, you might be a little curious about what was happening to your body. In case of a terminology emergency, turn to the glossary in the back of this book for instant assistance.

The only downside to her reading all these books is that, well, she'll expect you to read them, too. Of course, you're reading *this* book so that you don't have to read hers. Still, you need to know how to answer the question, "Why aren't you reading *my* book?"

$\mathscr{5}$ READING HER BOOK

There are very few things you can count on during pregnancy. One of those sure things is that your partner will want you to read her pregnancy tome.

This book is usually about 400 to 500 pages long and contains a number of drawings of various parts of a woman's body, which guys would normally find quite exciting. However, these drawings are so . . . *medical*.

Let's admit it. We don't want to think about our partner's body that way. Sure, after the baby is born, you may relent and adopt a more mature perspective. But at this stage, you're still clinging to a much less matronly image of your partner.

Here's how the Pregnancy Book Dance works:

1. She gets a really big pregnancy book.
2. She suggests you read it, too.
3. She proceeds to read about a hundred pages the first night.
4. She reads boring excerpts to you and then shows you really gross drawings of women's organs, convincing you to never look at this book again.
5. You never look at the book again.
6. She accuses you of not caring and asks why you're not "involved" in the pregnancy.
7. You feel like a failure—but still not a bad enough failure to be willing to endure her book to make the pain go away!

Some guys will do better than others in the Pregnancy Book Dance: You may find that you are a three-chapter guy, or maybe only two. Some guys don't make it past the front and back jacket covers. And a few recognize the cover by sight but couldn't tell you the title.

GUY TALK

My wife was always a lot more into them than I was. If there was a problem, I'd take the book and try to troubleshoot. Like if there's a plumbing problem I might take out a plumbing book. But I never really read the books to prepare myself.
—Michael

This issue is difficult to resolve. Your partner deserves your appreciation and encouragement for the time she invests reading and learning about the physical and emotional changes that pregnancy causes. These books give women knowledge, comfort, and confidence during a period of dramatic physical and emotional change.

Men, on the other hand, experience few physical or hormone-based emotional reactions. For guys, pregnancy mostly affects their *relationship*.

I suggest three possible ways to help you survive the Pregnancy Book Dance without stepping on your partner's toes:

Read her entire book
You'll not only impress her socks off, you'll be as knowledgeable as she is about what she's going through. The only negative is that you'll give other guys everywhere a bad rap.

Read this book
That's why I wrote it—so you would not have to read her book. Of course, you must read this book in the presence of your partner. You get no points if she does not actually see you reading it. For bonus points, read her an occasional excerpt.

Talk with her about why you're struggling with her book
Expectant moms naturally want their partner's involvement. The pregnancy guide seems like such an obvious and necessary resource that they don't understand when we don't join in their enthusiasm for reading it.

If this is an issue for you, try talking to your partner about what makes the book uncomfortable or uninteresting to you. She might surprise you and agree that most of the book is more relevant for her. And you might surprise yourself by discovering that there is usually one very good chapter devoted exclusively to guys in every women's pregnancy book.

The bottom line is that pregnant women believe in a Mandatory Minimum Requirement for Male Participation, or "MMRMP," which is the muffled objection that men make when offered her book. You can choose the "how," but you must meet this requirement.

part

TWO

2

SYMPTOMS

PHYSICAL SYMPTOMS

You are going to hear a lot about your partner's symptoms. You could dismiss her as a whiner, but this will only lead to additional complaints—complaints that you don't listen to her complaints. You can see where this path leads.

If you want to be able to sympathize with her in the way that she expects, you need to learn a little about what her body is going through. Now hold on a minute. I realize that you are reading this book rather than one of her pregnancy manuals because you don't *want* to learn any of that gross medical stuff. Don't worry. I promise to leave out the graphic explanations and mood-killing diagrams.

But let's face it. Your partner's body is going to change dramatically, and you had a lot to do with it.

What you need to know is that for every visible change you see, she is experiencing many more that you can't see but that she certainly feels.

And you'll hear about how she feels, I guarantee. Since we're guys and won't ever have to go through any of this ourselves, the least we can do is try to empathize with what it must be like for our partners. Here are common symptoms that accompany pregnancy.

BY THE NUMBERS

Most common symptoms reported by pregnant women

1. Frequent urination	89%	6. Cravings	56%
2. Fatigue	82%	7. Sleep loss	51%
3. Weight gain	79%	8. Swelling	51%
4. Nausea	66%	9. Sensitivity to smell	49%
5. Sore back	61%	10. Food aversions	42%

Morning Sickness

Remember how you felt Sunday morning after that Saturday-night keg party in college? Now imagine having a fraternity party *every* night for weeks. That's what it's like for many pregnant women when they get out of bed in the morning. And she never even had the pleasure of the night-before buzz, or dancing on speakers—nothing!

Think about that. The hangover without the party. Every day for weeks. Think about how cheerful you are when you have a hangover, then pick those socks up off the floor.

Morning sickness is a misnomer, too. Your partner may also experience afternoon sickness and evening sickness. This feeling of nausea is most common in the first few months and rarely lasts past the third month of pregnancy. The good news is that about half of all pregnant women do not feel nauseous at all during pregnancy. Count your partner and yourself lucky if she's one of them.

Gotta Go

"I need to *pee!*" your partner will say, with greater passion and greater frequency.

Put away your bladder-control jokes for these next nine months. If you had a baby pressing on *your* uterus—if you even *had* a uterus (and knew where and what it was)—you would need to pee really bad, too.

Fortunately, this greater need to pee is mainly during the first trimester and then again in the final month, when there's just not enough room for baby *and* bladder.

Cravings

At some point just about everyone has had a case of the "munchies," but even the most gluttonous of your late-night eating binges may not have prepared you for the cravings experienced by your pregnant partner.

Never question a craving. Consider yourself lucky if your wife's oddest wish is for healthy Mexican food.

One expectant mom went to the store for olives and emptied a jumbo jar of thirty-five olives before she made it home.

Less well known than food cravings are food aversions. Almost as many pregnant women develop a strong distaste for at least one food item that they liked before they became pregnant.

You may also see your formerly health-conscious partner lust after grease. As long as she's also eating the good stuff, try not to worry.

Remember, a craving is never wrong. It might be weird and even a little sick, but she wants what she wants. Your job is to get it for her.

Fatigue

Your partner is tired. Yeah, you're thinking, I get tired, too.

No. You don't understand. Before the baby, she worked all day and then came home and did all the things you would do if you weren't, well, a guy. And she never complained about being tired. So now, when she says she's tired, she's *really* tired.

Or, as one mom explained to me, you would be tired too if you were creating a life-support system from scratch inside *your* body!

There's also a selfish reason for you to be sympathetic. Within nine months, you'll join her pooped-out party. After your baby is born, you will discover degrees of sleep deprivation you thought were reserved for military torture. You will crawl off to work in the morning after a night of multiple feedings or nonstop crying and you'll wonder why anyone would willingly choose to have a second child.

So if you hope to get *any* sympathy at all from her later, you'd better be supportive of her complaints now. One day soon, you'll know firsthand that she wasn't kidding.

GIRL TALK

This is not a time to be saying, "Do you really need those french fries?" I'm telling you, yes, I really need those french fries!
—Janice

You might have thought your partner was moody *before* she became pregnant. Think again.

Here are a few of the signs that your partner may be especially sensitive:

- The "Kodak Moment" commercials bring tears to her eyes.
- You find her slumped over the kitchen counter, crying. When you ask what's wrong, she sobs that she burnt the toast.
- When you comment that she seems a little "moody," she shouts back, "*Moody? Who are you* calling *moody?*"

Pregnant women cannot deny their physical changes. However, expectant moms can be understandably sensitive about their emotional state.

These mood swings are not her fault. She's being bounced around by her hormones like a ball in a pinball machine. She can't help herself, so try to be patient. Telling her that she is moody can have the unintended effect of making her even more emotional. Women hate it when guys dismiss their feelings as a product of hormones, even when they're not pregnant.

Not all women display these heightened cycles of emotional highs and lows. If your partner is one of them, consider yourself fortunate. And if she *does* seem moody to you, try to find out if there's something specific wrong. Ask questions and you may uncover a specific issue or problem you can resolve. Just by asking and listening, you will have helped.

GIRL TALK

Our hormones are raging. They are raging, OK? We'll be super happy one day and crying the next. Guys need to understand that there's not a reason for it, that it's just the way we are during pregnancy.
—*Nancy*

Guys are caught up in myths about pregnancy. The second that I have a bad day...I was not *emotional! He* was *making* me *emotional by saying I was emotional!*
—*Carrie*

8 SYMPATHY PAINS

Congratulations. You are indulging your partner's cravings, listening supportively to her various bodily complaints, and pretending she isn't moody.

Being a modern, sensitive kind of guy, you are probably starting to say to yourself, "Hey, what about *me?*"

For example, you may be feeling more stressed, more emotional, and even having an upset stomach once in a while. Guess what? You're . . . *pregnant!*

Let me clarify. You are *not* pregnant. But some guys become so involved in their partner's pregnancy that they begin to feel some of the same physical and emotional swings as their partner.

Experts refer to these "sympathy" pains as couvade syndrome. Most pregnant women prefer a simpler term: *wimp*.

Could you be experiencing couvade syndrome? Research suggests that most men experience at least one of the symptoms associated with pregnancy but that only one in ten men suffer from couvade syndrome.

Surprisingly enough, men who complain to their partners about "feeling" pregnant are *not* showered with sympathy! Let's try to deduce why this syndrome would not be popular with pregnant women.

She is experiencing vomiting, sleeplessness, weight gain, bizarre cravings, and mood swings because there is a baby growing inside her body.

What's your excuse? (Long silent pause here.)

So you get the point. If you are genuinely experiencing physical or emotional reactions that concern you, consult your doctor for expert advice. But until or unless a doctor tells you otherwise, you might not

GIRL TALK

He'll complain that his back is hurting a little bit, or he has to go give blood. I think to myself, "Maybe you should try being pregnant."
—*Carrie*

want to spend a lot of time trying to convince your partner that you "know" what she's going through.

Nowhere is this more true than in reference to her weight. You know she's pregnant. She knows she's pregnant. Pregnant women gain weight. It sounds so simple. It's not.

part

THREE

③

LOOKING GOOD, FEELING GOOD

9 "DO I LOOK FAT?"
AND OTHER TRICK QUESTIONS

Approximately ten seconds after your partner realizes she is beginning to "show," she will begin to badger you with what I consider *Trick Questions*.

Let me illustrate with what appears to be an innocent exchange yet in fact contains the most lethal of all Trick Questions: "Do I look fat?"

Her: Do I look fat?
You: Nah, you look great.
Her: Oh, you're just saying that. I feel huge!
You: Well, of course you're bigger. You're pregnant.
Her: Ugh! So you *do* think I look *fat*! (She starts crying...)
You: "What did I say?"

The *truth*, silly. You told the truth.

You will find that Trick Questions share certain characteristics:

1. Your partner already knows the answer before she asks.
2. You are expected to tell her what she wants to hear, *not* the truth.
3. After you tell her what she wants to hear, she will try to talk you into telling the truth.
4. She still does not want you to tell the truth, and if you change your answer, she will be devastated.

Most of the time, telling the truth in relationships is a good thing. During pregnancy, however, some of the time-tested rules of communication—like being honest, for example—don't always apply.

Women take weight gain more personally than men. When men gain weight they often tell themselves that the extra weight makes them appear "more solid" or more mature. To the delight of manufacturers of baseball caps and sweats, guys really don't worry a lot about their appearance—much to the chagrin of their partners.

Women, on the other hand, are not amused by this transformation of their belly into a bowling ball. They worry that these changes to their appearance will change how you see them and change how you feel toward them. They don't feel as attractive or desirable. They don't feel as good about themselves. They worry they won't be able to lose all the weight after the baby is born. Their clothes don't feel or look good anymore.

What your partner needs from you is reassurance, *not* confirmation of her fears. She *knows* she is bigger. What she *doesn't* know is whether it matters to you. This is a great gift you can give to her, and you should volunteer it liberally, even if it means lying like a politician.

Personally, I recommend practicing because—let's face it—there will be a point where it will be darned hard to keep a straight face during one of these Trick Questions.

The good news is, nature will help you. You may be delighted to discover that you appreciate your partner in new ways, and you may notice a "glow" about her that makes her even more attractive to you in her new role as mother and life-giver. Let her know early and often if you feel that way. In the interim, *lie like crazy!*

Here are a few possible responses:

"Pregnancy really becomes you."
"I never imagined how beautiful you'd be pregnant."
"You really have a glow about you."
"If I didn't know, I'd never guess you were pregnant."
"I don't think you're showing at all."
"You've never looked more radiant."

More Tricks

Her concerns about weight gain can trigger a wide range of related Trick Questions. Here are the most common ones, and the necessary responses:

"Do you think I'm showing?"	(No!)
"Do you still find me attractive?"	(Yes!)
"Do you think I'm overreacting?"	(No!)

In a low moment, she may even ask, "Do you still love me?" Of course you do, so you might think this would be an easy one. The problem with Trick Questions is, even when you give the correct answer (in this case, "Yes"), you can still get in trouble if you are not quick enough or sincere enough!

To summarize, the proper response to Trick Questions is, *Lie if the truth hurts.*

Unfortunately, merely lying is not good enough. You must be convincing and persistent. Not only will she ask you a Trick Question, *not* wanting to hear the truth, but when you respond with your lie, she'll *argue* with you and try to convince you of the truth (which you already know to be true), yet you must persevere and keep insisting upon the lie more forcefully than she insists on the truth she doesn't want to hear.

That's why they're called Trick Questions.

GIRL TALK

He was great about telling me that I looked beautiful and that I had a "glow." I highly recommend that. Even if she says, "I do not—I look fat, my face is bloated, and my feet are puffed up," just persevere and keep insisting!
—Janice

WEIGHT GAIN AND CLOTHES GAIN

"I have *nothing* to wear." You've heard it a million times.

As early as the first trimester, her clothes will begin to feel tight and uncomfortable. By the middle trimester, her pre-pregnancy outfits simply won't fit.

To most women, this is a *big* deal. As the prevalence of Trick Questions proves, expectant moms feel understandably insecure about their appearance. Clothes that don't fit add to their anxiety.

Before long, the only thing left that fits will be her sweats. This might sound pretty appealing to the average guy. We would be perfectly content to lie around the house all weekend in sweats. But try your best to imagine how distressing it is for your partner to suddenly not fit into any of her clothes.

For her part, she'll do her best to help you understand the gravity of this problem.

Of course, maternity shops sell clothes designed to expand when and where she expands. However, they charge what may seem to you to be a hostage-taker's ransom for such temporary style and comfort. Your partner may long for outfits that flatter her inflating figure yet balk at the price tags in these specialty stores.

There are several ways you can offer wardrobe assistance. If your finances permit, buy her a gift certificate to a maternity store. She'll get the clothes she wants without feeling guilty. If cost is an issue, try talking to friends who've been pregnant recently who are similar in size. They'll have barely-used outfits and may be willing to help.

GIRL TALK

Clothes are important to me. I work, and it matters to me to look professional. When it came to buying maternity clothes, Bruce thought I was forgetting that pregnancy only lasted nine months. He would ask me, "Are you sure you need all those clothes?"
—Nancy

We are pregnant. We are carrying your child. We will wear—and spend—what we want to!
—Janice

Also, you could contact stores that specialize in used maternity wear. The handy thing about pregnancies is that they're sure to be over in about nine months, so these outfits won't be very worn. Pregnancy clothes are like fruitcakes. As long as everyone keeps passing them around, there's no need for any new ones.

You might think maternity clothes are your partner's problem. However, her weight gain can have a dramatic effect on how she feels about herself. How she feels about herself can have a dramatic effect on the level of romance in your relationship. In addition, her clothes influence her self-image. She may still look attractive to *you*, but she may not feel romantic unless she feels attractive, and comfortable clothes can help.

Shopping, anyone?

Will She Lose the Weight?

Guys may not care about their own clothes or weight, but we often pay quite a bit of attention to our partner's appearance. It is natural to wonder how much weight your partner will gain and whether she'll lose all the weight after the baby is born.

These are natural concerns. After all, it's hard for the average woman to hide thirty extra pounds. In addition, most women need months to return to their pre-pregnancy weight.

If her weight gain concerns you, here's some good news: It probably concerns her, too. Women are just as interested as their partners in regaining that pre-pregnancy figure.

The most helpful way to handle your own and her weight concerns is to reassure her, even as her body expands, that you love *all* of her.

BY THE NUMBERS

Desirable pregnancy weight gain for a normal-sized woman is twenty-five to thirty-five pounds.

BREASTS

Breasts. Let's face it. Guys like breasts. We've been known to stare at them. Women even claim that we *speak* to their breasts.

OK, fine. We admit it. Men, as a rule, are fascinated with women's breasts.

Now imagine if there were a safe, natural, and low-cost way of enhancing your partner's breasts? There is, and the procedure is called *pregnancy*.

BY THE NUMBERS

During the course of pregnancy, a woman's breasts can grow as much as three cup sizes.

Pregnancy naturally augments women's breasts. No implants, no big check to write. Just bigger breasts.

As early as the first month of pregnancy, you'll notice your partner's profile perking up. This can be quite exciting for the guy.

Before you get too excited, though, remember that this pleasant transformation is not for your benefit. There is actually a procreative purpose for her breasts to enlarge. They will soon become functional feeding machines. For many women, that means hands-off for you!

You heard me right. At the very moment that your partner's breasts are going to be larger and more desirable than ever before, you might not be allowed to touch them.

GIRL TALK

We're at a party and he's had a few beers and I hear him say, "She's so great, she's blown out of two bras already!" He was so proud of me, like I'm some major trophy!
—*Carrie*

The main reason why your partner's enhanced breasts may become off-limits is because they hurt. This swelling process makes her breasts especially sensitive. Therefore, during the first few months, these enhanced assets may be better seen than touched. You should take your lead from your partner.

By the middle trimester, the painfulness in her breasts normally subsides. However, your fascination with her breasts probably has not! So, the burning question in your mind may be, "Can I touch them, *please?*"

In fact, in the middle trimester your partner may find that her breast sensitivity enhances her enjoyment of lovemaking. Since every pregnancy is different, be sure to talk with your partner, expressing your desires and asking about her comfort and interest.

Second base has never looked this attractive before. Maybe you'd like to try for a home run?! You are now ready for the answer to the ultimate question about sex during pregnancy: Is there any?

BY THE NUMBERS

Breast changes reported by pregnant women

Larger	93%
Darkening of the areola	70%
Veins	52%
Leakage	43%
Increased sensation	41%

12 SEX!

Hellooooo? Anybody hoooome?

For some men, that deafening silence is their nonexistent sex life in the first few months after pregnancy. Let's face it. Your partner is too busy feeling nauseous, eating for two, and sleeping all the time to have either the energy or appetite for romance.

You could wallow in this lack of lovemaking. However, a more constructive use of your time would be to join a gym and start working on improving your endurance.

In the second trimester, something remarkable often happens. Your partner's hormones start raging and *she wants you!*

To your shock, and then to your delight, your partner may be "in the mood" more often during the middle three months than she was before she became pregnant. At this point, you'll be glad you've been doing your sit-ups. I also recommend a vitamin supplement.

In addition, women may enjoy sex more during this phase of pregnancy. Some women experience orgasms, or multiple orgasms, for the first time. (If your partner has been faking it for years, she might forget to mention this to you.)

Ironically, at this stage, you may find that you are the reluctant sexual partner. True, this contradicts the macho stereotype of guys always wanting sex more than women. However, many expectant dads are nervous that sexual intercourse will hurt their partner or the baby.

The good news is that you have nothing to worry about. From a purely clinical perspective, you are not putting your partner or your baby at risk by having sex during pregnancy. And if she's in the mood, it's great for your relationship.

I was one of
those "don't touch
me" women during
pregnancy. I think a
lot of it was I just
didn't feel attractive.
I know the books
say that some
women feel more in
the mood for part of
pregnancy. Not me.
I felt bad for him,
but I was honest
with him about
how I felt.
—Nancy

He was a little
nervous. I tried to tell
him, "Honey, you
can't get me preg-
nant again!" He was
like, "Oh, I dunno . . .
I don't want to
hurt the baby."
—Carrie

You might think,
"This stud is out
to pasture." No,
you're not. You are
back in service!
—Janice

Your body
releases some
sort of a "come and
get me" hormone!
I was like, "Honey,
come on over to my
side of the bed!"
—Carrie

Still, it is common for guys to feel awkward and more hesitant about sex. If it's not out of concern for mom and the baby, it can be because your partner's body has changed. Sure, her breasts are larger, but so are other parts of her body. If you're having trouble seeing her in the same sexual light, take comfort in knowing that you're not alone.

BY THE NUMBERS

In a survey of pregnant women, 29 percent described their sex habits during the third trimester as "only in my dreams."

Even if your appetite for romance remains healthy, hers will likely ebb and flow. By the third trimester, hormonal changes and increasing physical distress typically result in a waning of your partner's interest in lovemaking. In the last month, the only moaning you hear may be her lamenting the fact that she's *still* pregnant.

What's "Normal"?

In general, what's normal about sex during pregnancy is that nothing is normal. Your pre-pregnancy frequency of lovemaking may drop or increase. Each of you may experience greater or lesser degrees of arousal at different times during pregnancy. You and especially your partner may experience *more* pleasurable intercourse.

Talking with your partner about your desires and asking her about hers is what works best, because so much about sex is unpredictable during these nine months.

BY THE NUMBERS

How women's sexual desires matched their mate's during pregnancy

Same	41%
Man wanted sex more often	36%
Woman wanted sex more often	23%

4

LET'S GET
MEDICAL

WHERE TO GIVE BIRTH

By now, there's no denying that you're going to be having a baby. A major decision is *where* you want to deliver your baby and *who* you want to perform the delivery. You'll want to consider your options before you make that initial doctor's visit.

The majority of deliveries happen in hospitals and are done by doctors. But there are other options you may want to evaluate. Each has its own advantages and drawbacks.

Hospital Births

Most women have their babies in hospitals. Expectant moms usually choose hospitals for their delivery because they feel safest there. Especially for first-time parents, this can be a great source of comfort during what can be a frightening experience.

A hospital delivery is an especially wise choice if there have been complications or are risk factors associated with your pregnancy.

Hospitals, for their part, continue to try to create a more comfortable and "homey" feel in their delivery units. Many hospitals now offer suites with room for dad to crash on the couch, and the delivery takes place in your hotel-like room.

Birthing Centers

Birthing centers are staffed by midwives and offer a comfortable setting that feels more like your own home than a hospital. Couples are encouraged to be actively involved at every stage from childbirth education through labor and delivery. Birth centers typically will prescreen clients to ensure that they accept only safe, low-risk pregnancies and will refer or transfer a couple to a hospital if the pregnancy becomes risky.

Home Births

Giving birth at home offers moms the comfort and familiarity of their normal surroundings instead of the medical feeling of a hospital. Comfort aids are more readily available and a home birth is more conducive to family participation. This choice is more common for second-time parents who have already been through labor and delivery once in a hospital.

Water Births

Delivering the baby in a birthing pool is also an option at some birthing centers. A few hospitals even offer this option. Advocates cite the freedom of movement and buoyancy of the birthing pool as well as the calm atmosphere. Consult your physician.

Nurse-Midwife Deliveries

Doctors deliver most babies, but nurse midwives are a popular alternative. Nurse midwives are specifically trained to work with expectant moms through all the stages of pregnancy. They will often work in the more casual environment of a birthing center, but some hospitals also have nurse midwifes available.

Women who choose and enjoy this option appreciate the closer relationship that exists with a nurse midwife than might normally exist with a doctor.

For resources in your area, see the bibliography and resources in the back of this book.

Choosing Among Birthing Options

Typically, your partner will already know and make clear to you her preferences regarding where and how she delivers. Since she's the one who will take the physical risks and do the physical labor, her vote is the one that counts.

Be aware, however, that if your partner has a pregnancy that is high-risk in any way, a hospital delivery with a supervising doctor is the safest approach. Consult with a medical professional you trust before selecting options that limit your access to medical assistance in the event of an unexpected emergency.

Before making your final choice, take a tour of the locations you're considering. Look at their rooms and imagine how you'd both feel there. Talk to other patients and ask them about their experiences. Most important, interview the person who'll provide your care. Be sure that their philosophy and practices match your own.

Once you've determined where and how you'll have your baby delivered, you're ready for the offer you can't refuse: "Will you come to my doctor's appointments with me?"

Another Mandatory Minimum Requirement of Male Participation is that you go with her to her doctor's appointments.

Do you *have* to go? Think of it this way. These visits aren't optional for *her*. Why should you get off the hook?

As guys, we have lots of good and logical reasons for not going on these visits. Most things medical make us queasy, we don't understand any of the terms doctors and nurses use, and we can't actually *do* anything, anyway. No one is interested in taking *our* blood or checking *our* heartbeat. Besides, we're busy with work. Oh yeah, and other guys don't go with their partners.

All this may be true. It doesn't matter. You're going.

And as far as responsibilities go, this one is a piece of cake. You don't have to say or do anything except *be there*, and it's OK if you're confused by what the doctors are saying.

You will score *big points* with your partner just by being present. You'll even earn bonus points if you're the only guy in sight during the visit. And in case you haven't realized it by now, you need to stock up on points every chance you get.

The Invisible Male Syndrome

It's ironic that everyone considers it so important that you accompany your partner to her doctor's office—because, once there, you may very well be treated as though you are *not there*.

Don't take this personally, or get insulted, or run out and start a guys' rights group. The truth is, everyone is

GUY TALK

I was required to go to every single one of them. I tried to get out of it a couple of times. Her argument was, "We're doing this together." I figured that she gets weighed in, the doctor asks how she's feeling, they listen to her tummy, and they send her home—why do I need to be there? I lost that argument every single time.
—John

just so darned shocked to see you actually show up that they don't quite know how to respond. So they ignore you.

My advice is to enjoy your anonymity. There are few times in our lives where we can be someplace and not be noticed, talked to, or asked questions. Savor your *invisibility*. Remember how many points you're scoring with your partner just by being there—even if she is apparently the *only* person who seems to be able to see you.

If you think *you* are uncomfortable, think of what it must be like for all those medical people who don't know what to say in front of a guy. Take pride in being a trailblazer for a future where it's normal for *all* involved to have the father accompany his partner for checkups.

There are a number of ways to amuse yourself during these visits:

- Keep track of how many times you hear Prego Lingo like *trimester, weeks,* and *baby* (no *the*).
- Flaunt your own Prego Lingo savvy by seeing how many of these terms you can needlessly work into the conversation.
- Try to trick the hospital staff into discussing your partner's pregnancy in terms of *months*.
- Refer to as many other events as you can in terms of their Pregnancy Time equivalent (see chapter 4). For example: "Did you know we have only 936 more weeks to save for baby's college fund?"

Going with your partner to her doctor's appointments is one of the nicest (and easiest) things you can do to show your support for her.

In return, you will be rewarded by being present for one of life's most memorable moments—the first time you hear and see your baby.

GUY TALK

You walk in and people look at you like "there's a guy in here." And you can just feel the stares. And then we're in the room and the doctor engages in wonderful conversation with my wife, kind of looks at me like "Oh, hi," then goes back to my wife, semi-ignoring me. I was the invisible partner. I always made a point to be there, but I always got the same reaction. And my wife always wanted me to leave during the actual exams— which was kind of funny, because of course I was there at the delivery, and that was a whole lot more graphic!
—Michael

15   HEARING THE HEARTBEAT

If you can survive the onslaught of medical terms used at the doctor's office, you will be rewarded with a glimpse into the world of the womb, thanks to some miraculous medical toys.

The first of these is the fetal monitor. This is basically a fancy stethoscope. What makes it so cool is that it can be used to amplify your baby's heartbeat so you can hear it!

I'll never forget that moment. The doctor moved the amplifier around on my wife's belly until finally the static organized into a barely discernible yet distinct rumbling, regular beat. I cried and my wife laughed— two different expressions of the same feeling of wonderment and joy.

BY THE NUMBERS

The baby's heartbeat can be heard as early as ten or twelve weeks into pregnancy.

Even more impressive is the ultrasound. This device bounces sound waves off your partner's belly in much the same way that a whale bounces sounds off its environment to find its way around. (I swear I am *not* comparing pregnant women to whales. Shame on you for even thinking that.)

What results from this machine is a *picture* of the womb. Yes, you can actually watch your baby on

GUY TALK

The ultrasound was great. When I heard the heartbeat and saw the picture, we both cried. We could see its arms and legs pushing up and down, and we both could see it, and she could feel it at the same time.
—John

Seeing our baby for the first time on the ultrasound scanner was a magical experience. It helped us feel much more connected to our child as an impending individual.
—Paul

television. True, the picture will remind you of an old black-and-white television with bad reception. But this is one show where you'll never reach for the remote. Through all that black-and-white snow is the tiny yet clearly recognizable form of . . . your baby. If the baby is lying just right, you can see little baby legs and arms, and hands and head, and if the picture is clear enough, this could be your first opportunity to find out: boy or girl?

BY THE NUMBERS

Three-quarters of couples choose to find out the sex of their unborn baby.

Even if you decide you don't want to know the sex of your baby, you won't want to miss the opportunity to glimpse inside the womb to meet your unborn child.

Just when you think it can't get any better, the technician will offer you more: an actual photographic print of your unborn child. A few hospitals even provide you with a video cassette!

That's right, there's no need to wait until the birth anymore. You can begin subjecting your friends to baby pictures while your unborn child is still in the womb.

For many men, hearing the heartbeat and seeing their baby for the first time on the ultrasound are moments they cherish forever. These are moments that help make pregnancy as real for the man as it has been all along for his partner. Don't miss the chance to hear and see this life you've created.

ABSTAIN OR INDULGE:
THE DRINKING DILEMMA

Once you've heard your baby's heartbeat, you are likely to be more sensitive to your partner's health and lifestyle habits. After all, that little life inside the womb is dependent upon her to take good care of her body.

To her credit, your mate will most likely choose to abstain from drinking alcohol while carrying the baby. If she's unsure, encourage her to educate herself about the risks. Research shows that women who drink alcohol during pregnancy increase their odds of having a low-birth-weight baby.

For the sake of the baby, your partner will probably volunteer to become the "designated driver" for the duration of her term. Since you will still go out to social events together, you must decide how to handle this newfound freedom to drink.

Your options range from drinking yourself into a stupor at every event you attend and annoying your partner and everyone around you to joining your partner in abstaining and frowning upon anyone else who dares to drink in front of your fetus. You can see that failing to strike a balance between these extremes will leave you friendless and alone. The choice is up to you, but the degree to which you indulge will have predictable consequences for you.

For example, someone will undoubtedly come up to you at a party and joke that your partner is "eating for two." Being a guy, you may be tempted to chime in with "And I'm *drinking* for two." This is a good way to get that drink dumped on you. Remember, your partner can get away with practically anything because she is pregnant. Any goodwill toward you, however, is based completely on your acting the part of the caring and supportive father-to-be. Mess up this perception and start looking for a quiet corner or a comfortable bag to put over your head.

A smarter course of action might be to tell other party-goers, "We are pregnant," and order a soft drink. Your partner isn't the only one who'll be impressed.

If your goal is to help your mate make healthy choices during her pregnancy, you will make it much easier for her to abstain from alcohol if you do the same. Nine months is a long time. Her willpower and endurance will be tested. Your drinking choices can either ease her struggle or frustrate her further.

Of course, you can still drink when you're out alone with friends. And an occasional drink at parties won't drive your mate crazy with envy. But you'll make it a lot easier for her to do the right thing for your child if you join her in sacrifice.

The danger here is that, guys being guys, it is often not enough for us to make just a small sacrifice here and there. Once you begin to participate in safeguarding your baby's health, you may find it hard to stop. You might begin innocently enough by encouraging your partner not to drink alcohol, but before you know it, you're meddling in all her health affairs, and you've become a Dad-Nag.

17 THE DREADED DAD-NAG

Once you choose the high road of joining your partner in avoiding alcohol, you'll naturally start paying attention to other aspects of her health.

You might point out that those french fries she's shoveling into her mouth are rather high in fat. Or, gosh, you notice she hasn't taken time to exercise lately, so maybe the two of you should go for a stroll around the neighborhood. Or, my, she's staying up awfully late tonight—remember the *baby* needs its rest!

Of course, your intentions are honorable. You're just thinking of the baby, right? Good luck convincing *her* of that.

Chances are she will respond to your dietary advice by sarcastically thanking you for being the first person to ever tell her that french fries are fatty, because all her life she thought they were just a healthy way to add more starch to her diet.

She might take you up on your invitation for a stroll and appreciate your willingness to be her personal Richard Simmons. But she is more likely to use her walking shoes to beat you over the head. She'll see your offer as a not-so-subtle suggestion that she's too large. You may even experience the shock of her saying to you, "Stop *nagging* me!"

Clearly, you must walk that fine line between encouraging healthy habits and, well, being a pest.

Remember all the times your wife/girlfriend/mother asked you to do something you already promised to do but still hadn't done? For example, pick up your socks, take out the trash, do the dishes, make house repairs, put away the laundry, get a life—you get the point. Was that a *fun* experience? Of course not! So why should our partners give us hugs and kisses for implying that they are insensitive to their unborn child?

Obviously, nagging won't work. What you can do is gently lead by example. Go for daily walks at a time that's also convenient for your partner. Let her know she's always welcome to join you if she feels up to it.

Pregnant women should keep their heart rate below 140 beats per minute during exercise.

When you're at parties, moderate your drinking and she won't feel so deprived. When you're hungry, whether eating out or ordering in, choose healthier foods. The best thing you can do is treat yourself, and your mate, the way you'd like to see her treat herself.

It also wouldn't hurt to keep in mind that women are extraordinarily good at knowing what they and their baby need. After all, what are food cravings and aversions except a woman's body telling her she needs more or less of some type of nutrient? Be concerned. Be supportive. But remember, it's her body.

5

GETTING
ALONG

18 WHAT WOMEN REALLY WANT

What do women really want? Every modern guy puzzles over this question. Nor is this a new problem. Archaeologists have excavated early cave drawings of men scratching their heads, no doubt pondering the mystery of cave women.

Despite all the contemplation, men still wonder what women want. But women are pretty clear. In fact, pregnant women are more than willing to tell you what they want. They want your involvement, your support, and your understanding, of course.

Unfortunately, most guys aren't quite sure how that translates into *action*. So I've surveyed women about their pregnancy experiences and prepared this unscientific summary of the findings. Listen up, guys. Here's how pregnant women think:

Rule #1: I want what I want, when I want it
Whether it's money, sex, the baby's room, or her clothes, the pregnant woman operates by a different time standard: immediate gratification, without discussion.

Rule #2: I'm the one carrying the baby, and the least you can do is ...
This is the "Queen for a Day" rule that extends for nine months. You might balk and say, "That's too long to have it your way." This would be a good time to remember: It could be worse—*you* could be pregnant.

If you try to argue, you will quickly discover the corollary to rule #2: *Because I'm pregnant!* Pregnancy alone is an adequate rationale for whatever she decides or wants in the moment. No further analysis is necessary—or desired! It is pointless, for example, to state the obvious: "That's not logical." Logic is irrelevant.

Rule #3: Tell me what I want to hear, even if I argue with you
She's gained weight. You both know it. But when she asks, you simply must *know* that she expects you to tell her what she wants to hear.

Armed with this knowledge, you can now recover some of the points you've undoubtedly lost with a few specific actions that are sure to enchant your mate. Here are five things you can do to score points with your partner:

1. Tell her you still find her beautiful.
2. Give her massages.
3. Tell her you love her.
4. Give her flowers.
5. Give her a gift at delivery (see chapter 37 for ideas).

And for extra credit:

- Go with her to the wallpaper store.
- Alphabetize her spice rack.
- Buy her a "baby names" book.
- Let her catch you reading a chapter of *her* pregnancy book.

You will probably continue to think your partner is crazy, but by knowing her rules, you can keep those clashes to a minimum.

If you really want to clean up in the game of communication, you'll need to actually clean up. However, if you're like most guys, you're going to need some help yourself before you can help around the house.

HELPING WITH HOUSEHOLD CHORES—
FOR THE FIRST TIME?

You know why they call them "chores," don't you? If they were fun to do, they'd call them "games." When your partner gets pregnant, she can't do all the things around the house that she once did. You, being *the guy,* didn't even know half of what she did. You're about to find out.

The temptation here is to use the exact technique you have always used to get out of doing housework, which is to screw up whatever you are doing so badly that she will beg you never to help with that particular chore again. Remember, this time you really do need to help, and doing it wrong will only cause her more stress.

Most men capable of keeping a partner these days have rudimentary knowledge of common household chores. In case you are a little rusty when it comes to helping out around the house, here is "A Guy's Primer to Household Chores."

Laundry

You've got your washer, you've got your detergent, you've got your dryer. What could be simpler? Ha! Forget those college days of dumping all your clothes into the washer and pumping it full of quarters. Welcome to the world of small/medium/large loads, cold-cold/warm-cold/warm-warm, and normal/heavy/permanent-press cycles. Did I mention bleach and pre-soaking? Today's washing machines make the dry cleaner look like a bargain. The biggest potential problem for guys is washing exotic fabrics— such as anything that is not cotton. If you're not sure, ask. Don't find out the hard way that you shouldn't put rayon in the dryer.

Before you dump whites and colors together in the same load, sit your mate down and explain that you are *laundry-impaired* and need her help. I had my wife write out lists of which things go in which groups: "Jeans with darks, warm-cold, normal."

Some women are quite particular about how they want their laundry done, and others don't care as long as their clothes are approximately the same color and size after washing as they were before. Know what your partner expects and do the best job you possibly can.

Dishes

Wash them *before* putting them in the dishwasher. I realize this flies in the face of all common sense. After all, it's called a dish*washer*, not a dish *rinser*. But your partner will make you wash them by hand afterwards if the glasses wind up spotted, so never put anything in the dishwasher that isn't already clean.

Vacuuming

As with laundry, vacuuming seems simple on the surface, but in fact your partner knows that there are subtle and sophisticated techniques for sweeping across your carpets and rugs. Some women are devoted to the cross-cut. Others go for the long parallel sweep. Interview your partner on her preferred vacuuming strategies before you try this task, or risk discovering what happens when your carpet lines fail to overlap.

Picking Stuff Up

You have to do it. And not just your own mess. You even have to pick up stuff you didn't drop. Now you know how she felt all those years.

If it helps, pretend you're on a camping trip. You've always followed the camper's code—"Pack it in, pack it out"—when you were in the woods. Why not treat your own home as well as you treat the state park?

Cleaning the Bathroom

Hire a maid. Really, it won't cost that much. Besides, you *know* what you do in the bathroom. Would you rather clean it yourself or pay a complete stranger a few extra bucks?

Your other alternative, of course, is to aim more carefully in the first place. Like I said, hire a maid.

20   TOSSING AND TURNING

In the second half of pregnancy, your bed will be a busy place. Pillows will be flying and sheets will be askew, all because of your partner's passionate efforts to . . . find a comfortable sleeping position. Sorry.

As your partner expands, she finds it harder and harder to sleep. So she flips. And flips. And flips. Of course, when she was just your svelte bedmate she did this, too. But now she's flipping for two, and the after-shocks could leave you sleepless.

Here are your options:

1. Complain that she's tossing and turning so much, finishing with "How do you expect *me* to get any sleep?"
2. Any other response.

So option #1 it is. But surely there must be something you can do other than lie there suffering silently. The most extreme and therefore most effective solution is to flee to another bed!

I know this sounds unromantic. Sleeping in different rooms is for our grandparents, right? But if you're going to be the supportive partner you strive to be, you need to be well-rested. This is probably not something you want to make a habit of, but if you have a big day coming up at work or you are just unbearably exhausted, it might be a good idea. You might both be more comfortable, since she probably feels somewhat guilty for keeping you awake. On nights when she's tossing and turning, you'll help one another by snoozing separately.

There are, of course, less drastic compromises. I suggest you invest in a variety of pillows. Surprise her one night with a grab bag of those little square and round ones. She can mix and match until she finds that perfect sleeping combination.

Also, try to view these turbulent nights as training for parenthood. If you think it's hard to sleep while your partner tosses and turns, wait until your baby arrives. Soon, you'll long for those nights when the solution to your sleep deprivation was as simple as changing beds. The moment you become a parent, you will develop a sensitivity so acute that you'll awaken at the slightest sound from your newborn.

Eventually, of course, both you and your baby will sleep through the night. In the interim, learn to take naps without guilt, buy a few extra pillows, and change the sheets in the guest bedroom.

BOYS' NIGHT OUT

R-r-ring. You answer the phone. Your buddies are all meeting at the usual place to tilt some brews and shoot some pool. "C'mon down," says your friend.

You look at your pregnant partner. She's not having a good day. You hesitate. "Uh . . . I dunno . . ." you mumble back. "Maybe . . . next time, OK?" You hang up.

Of course, she wants to know all the details: "Who was that?" . . . "Why was he calling?" . . . "Oh." Pause.

Then, as sure as she is pregnant, she'll say, "If you really want to, you can go join them."

You get a little bit excited, imagining that cold beer mug, the laughter, the crack of the cue ball on the break.

"Really?"

"Sure . . . I'll be fine all alone here by myself."

Zing! You *fell* for it.

The pity pours over you like a wave, dousing your hopes of a guilt-free evening with the boys.

You're stuck. On the one hand, you could still go ahead and join your pals. But you know you'll be so stricken with guilt that you won't have any fun. Or you can stay home, resenting being stuck inside while your friends cavort.

You can avoid this trap, and you need to try. Preserving Boys' Night Out is vital to your emotional health. After all, you've put most of your effort into supporting your partner's needs. You also need to make time for yourself. Otherwise, you may begin to resent your partner or the baby.

Guilt-free get-togethers with the guys will require understanding and planning. First of all, recognize that your mate isn't being mean when she wants you to stay home. She has less energy and less mobility. She wishes she could go out and enjoy herself, but in reality, going out sounds more like a chore to her. Her idea of a social life right now might be you and a movie on the VCR.

Naturally, she envies your freedom from the physical symptoms that drain her energy. You, being the guy, are *not* pregnant. You are not tired. When you go out on the town and stay out late, it's just another reminder that guys have it easy.

You *can* have fun with the guys without leaving your partner feeling left out if you plan ahead and take the initiative.

Early in her pregnancy, offer to reduce the number of times you see the guys. Ask her for her input. Is she comfortable with you going out once every two weeks, or every three weeks?

She will appreciate being asked, and she'll be grateful for your willingness to compromise. You'll benefit because you'll probably wind up seeing your friends *more* than if you wait until it becomes a source of conflict. You'll also be able to *enjoy* those get-togethers more because they will be "pre-approved."

In return for this freedom that your partner gives you, think of comparable ways to repay her. Encourage her to still do a "girls' night out," even if it's less frequent than before her pregnancy. All the better if her night out and yours coincide, because this is one of the last times you will both be able to go out at the same time without having to arrange for a babysitter. Or, if going out really isn't appealing, suggest she invite her friends over, or bring her a "care package" she can enjoy at home. You could also give her a gift certificate for a pampering pedicure or manicure.

By anticipating this conflict, you can take care of your own needs as well as your partner's.

22 MOTHER-IN-LAW

Shortly after you announce that you're pregnant, your mother-in-law will come for a visit. The same law of nature that sends birds south for the winter, homing pigeons home, and salmon upstream to spawn sends mothers to their expectant daughters. Some arrive months in advance.

Brace yourself. Mothers, when their daughters become pregnant, are overcome by the need to give advice. Yes, even more advice than normal.

Pregnancy is also when a mother-in-law realizes that you and her daughter have reached the point of relationship no-return. You really are going to be with her for a while. This sets off all kinds of primal alarms that pretty much reduce to this statement: "You are *not* good enough for *my daughter.*"

Mothers-in-law are much more skillful communicators, though, so they'll be able to find five or more different ways of making this point—perhaps all in one visit.

By the end of her visit, you'll wonder how you ever found your way to work in the morning or even tied your shoes.

You will quickly learn that a mother-in-law has *all* the answers. Unfortunately, her answers usually turn out to be just the opposite of what you and your partner had planned to do.

If you are dumb enough to tell her you disagree, you're doomed. Your best bet is just to try to listen and repeat back her recommendations. Wait until she leaves, and then agree together to ignore everything! If you reveal your plans to break Mom's rules, you will sentence yourself to far more than nine months of reprisals.

GUY TALK

In preparation for the blessed event, the birth of our baby, the mother-in-law arrived approximately seven weeks in advance! We had live-in parents-in-law for seven weeks.
—*John*

Here's what you'll be *tempted* to say:

"Hey, you *had* your chance already."
"I married her, didn't I? Isn't that good enough for you?"
"Don't you have other children you could be visiting?"
"Butt out."

GUY TALK

My mother-in-law was telling me how it should be done. "I've had two children, Kevin," she'd say. I tried to tell her, "You gotta understand those were your children. This is my child." She was telling me how it had to be done. And I have a nice mother-in-law. I respect her and like her. And we still got into it.
—Kevin

Both sets of parents were a big help. We were really glad to have them around.
—Mike

Here's what you should say instead:

"Gee, mom-in-law name here, I can see why you did it that way."
"I'm glad that method worked so well for you."
"I really appreciate how concerned you are for the welfare of our baby."

Remember, laughing out loud will diminish the effectiveness of your remarks.

If it's any consolation, know that your mother-in-law may actually wind up irritating your wife even more than she irritates you. At least you're only related to her by marriage.

On the other hand, many dads are pleasantly surprised by, and very appreciative of, their mother-in-law during those first weeks after the baby is born.

Let's face it. Your parents have been there before and you haven't. Mom and Dad's experience can be a real asset. Besides, it's nice to have an extra pair of trusted hands around during those early sleepless weeks.

If your mother-in-law is getting to you, try to remind yourself that she means well. You can't really get too mad at someone who cares so much about your partner. Well, OK, you *can*, but it won't help.

Part of the reason mothers-in-law can upset new and expectant dads is that they fuel our growing fears that ... they may be *right*. What if we are *not* cut out to be dads?

IMMEDIATE OPENING—"PARENT"

JOB DESCRIPTION
HOURS: 16 hours daily, 7 days a week (nights on demand). DUTIES: Feed, clothe, bathe, rock, carry, change diapers, discipline, praise, entertain, educate, impart values. DURATION: Lifetime appointment. RETIREMENT: Doubtful.

For much of your partner's pregnancy, you have been focused on the immediate concerns: "How is she feeling?" and "How is her health?" and "What can (or should) I be doing?"

As you head into the home stretch, you'll likely be hit by an alarming thought: "I'm going to be a dad!"

Sure, you already know that. But for every expectant dad, there is a point during pregnancy when he "gets it," when he begins to visualize himself as a father. This can be a scary moment.

You may remember all the things your dad did or didn't do. Depending on your childhood experiences, you will likely say to yourself either "I hope I can be the kind of dad my father was" or "I hope I don't turn into the kind of dad my father was."

Expectant dads are right to worry. Your primary proven "qualification" for the job of parenting is that you are potent enough to impregnate your partner. Congratulations. Unfortunately, potency is not a particularly relevant skill once your child is born.

Now for the good news: Millions of other men (and women) with your same qualifications become parents each year. Most of them had more training to get their driver's license than to be parents. And they manage to do just fine.

Parenthood is the ultimate on-the-job training program. Nobody starts with any previous experience, yet everyone learns. You are surrounded by people who care about you and your success as a parent. Draw on your family and friends for their experiences, expertise, and opinions.

Then decide for yourself and trust your instincts. This system has worked pretty well for the last three thousand years or so.

GUY TALK

It was hard for me to accept the fact that I was going to be a father—and that suddenly I was going to have to grow up and be responsible. I also wanted to make sure that I'm a better father than my father was to me. I had a good father, but you always want to do better. I felt a real burden.
—Michael

part

SIX

6

GETTING
READY

THE BABY'S ROOM: "IS IT *DONE* YET?"

One of the inconvenient things about having a baby is that you'll need to find a place to put it. Even before you get pregnant, you and your partner will probably have planned which room will become the baby's room. Naturally, you will assume that you are therefore done with the issue of the baby's room. Naturally, you will be wrong.

Just past the halfway point in your partner's pregnancy, her baby-room alarm will go off. You'll know this because she'll start peppering you with pressing details like these: "Should we paint the walls or wallpaper them?" . . . "What firmness mattress should we get?" . . . "What color scheme should we use?"

Do *not* answer, "I don't care," even though you probably don't care. These questions are your advance warning that your partner has been overcome by Baby Room Frenzy. From this point on, she will obsess about whether you're going to complete the baby's room in time for the baby's arrival.

Your inclination will be to emphasize the obvious: "Honey, the baby's not due for four months."

Wrong answer. You are using the logical side of your brain, which is a good way to get in a big fight with your pregnant partner, who is using the Baby Room Frenzy side of her brain.

Like it or not, you are going shopping for the baby's room. Being a fiscally responsible kind of fellow, you'll undoubtedly ask yourself, Does a little baby *really* need all this stuff? Technically speaking, based on extensive research and cross-cultural data, no. But that's irrelevant. We're talking about *your baby*!

GUY TALK

To me it was like, no big deal, we'll get it done—we've got nine months.
—Mike

When it came to buying stuff for the baby, I learned to zip up my mouth and open up my wallet. Whatever she wants, she gets. If I mentioned the price, she'd say, "How can you bring up money when it's for our baby?"
—John

Remember that tip about buying your home-entertainment system *before* you got pregnant? Now you understand. Having a baby and being fiscally rational are pretty much mutually exclusive.

To survive Baby Room Frenzy, you'll need to do two additional things: First, feign interest in minute details while still letting your mate make *every* decision. For example, you might answer the wallpaper or paint quiz by saying, "I think wallpaper and paint would both be excellent choices, honey. I also agree it's an important decision. Which do *you* think would work better?"

Second, you'll need to complete every part of the baby-room conversion about three months sooner than seems necessary. Otherwise, your partner will be consumed by the fear that the room won't be ready in time. Don't be surprised if she says something like "Dear, the room isn't done and the baby will be here in just *three months!*" Or, she may challenge you with some hypothetical scenario like "Honey, what if I deliver eight weeks early?" Bite your tongue and do not laugh out loud. Just get the project done ahead of time.

My experience proves the value of obeying this advice. I dragged my feet finishing the baby's room and what happened? My wife had an emergency C-section and delivered our baby five weeks early. Take it from me, you don't want to be shopping for cribs after your baby is born.

GIRL TALK

If I heard one more time, "The baby's never gonna know what kind of room she's in . . ." If it wasn't for me that room would never have been done.
—*Carrie*

Pay attention to our nesting instincts. They are real. They are irrational but they are real. You will finish the baby's room, you will hang the paper we choose, you will assemble the baby's crib by the date we give you!
—*Janice*

GUY TALK

We argued over every piece of furniture in the room. We argued over the changing table. My point was, "Do we really need a changing table? What did they do until fifty years ago?" We got a changing table. Then we argued over the crib. I know our family. Sure enough, our daughter has never slept in her crib. Ever. I have a $250 crib, top of the line, with a special mattress, and she's never slept in it. She sleeps with us.
—*Kevin*

THE NAME GAME

25

Among the things you'll have to resolve much sooner than seems necessary to your guy brain is the question of your baby's name.

From "It" to "Bob"

There is a natural progression in the labeling of your child. When you first discover that you are going to have a baby, you'll probably refer to it as, well, "it."

"It" is quickly replaced by "baby." For the next few months, "baby" is specific enough. You both have a lot of other issues on your mind.

Then one day, you take that trip to the doctor and get to watch womb movies and play "Guess My Sex." From this point until you agree on a specific name, the baby will be "he" or "she."

Once you've reached the "he/she" stage, the Baby Name Game is right around the corner.

Types of Names

Men look at a painted wall and see "green." Women might see mint, teal, emerald, turquoise, or aquamarine.

This same phenomenon occurs with baby names. A guy who's having a boy will think of names like Bill, Bob, John, Mark, and Mike. These are solid guy names. His partner is more likely to suggest Colin or Brandon.

Fortunately, you are not the first couple who has struggled with the "What should we call our baby?" question. As a result, there are several books devoted entirely to listing possible names for your bundle of joy.

*Our biggest dis-
agreement was over
our daughter's
middle name.
I wanted her to
have an interesting
and unusual middle
name. I offered a
variety of long and
complicated German
names, Indian
names, Asian names.
My wife thought
they were all weird
and would trauma-
tize our child. Then
I started reading
Herodotus' history of
the ancient world
and stumbled onto a
treasure trove of
exotic Persian,
Greek, and Egyptian
names. I was clearly
making no progress,
and my wife led a
determined cam-
paign of organizing
support for her
position among
her friends and
women relatives.
Two weeks
before the birth,
I finally gave in.
Our daughter's
middle name is
"Jane."
—Paul*

These name books have several advantages. For example, it's helpful to know that the most popular boy's name is Michael or that hardly any girls—or boys—are actually named Peggy Sue.

However, there is a deeper danger buried within these books: too many choices!

Until you buy a baby-name book, your options are limited by your own imagination. This, of course, was no barrier to Frank Zappa, who named his children "Moon Unit" and "Dweezil." The rest of us are more likely to gravitate to favorite family names or the names of special people from our lives.

Once you buy a baby-name book, suddenly you have *thousands* of perfectly good names to choose from—with fractional differences to distinguish one from another.

This onslaught of choices threatens to prolong the Baby Name Game for months, potentially right up until delivery: "OK, honey, *Breath—two—three—four.* Hey, here's a good name on page 47…"

BY THE NUMBERS

Most popular baby names (1997)

	Boys	Girls
1.	Michael	Sarah
2.	Matthew	Emily
3.	Nicholas	Kaitlyn
4.	Jacob	Brianna
5.	Christopher	Ashley

Source: Michael Shackleford, A.S.A.; data from Social Security Administration.

Narrowing Your Choices

How do you break the gridlock when you reach name overload? The strategy you used to survive your partner's Baby Room Frenzy—let *her* decide—won't work here because guys actually care about their child's name.

Believe it or not, you will need to fall back on that well-known pre-pregnancy relationship strategy called *communication*. Each of you has an equal vote in selecting your child's name, and ideally you'd like to find common ground. But be prepared for an extended negotiation in search of that perfect name.

Here are some of the most common reasons partners pick, or nix, a name:

Names as destiny

There are entire baby-name books devoted to choosing a name that evokes a certain mood or spirit. You may or may not believe that a name determines your destiny. Nevertheless, your child will have this name for a really long time, so think about whether you want a strong or soft or neutral name. "Sue" and "Amanda" are both fine choices but evoke images of two very different personalities.

Nicknames are names, too

"William" might sound sophisticated, but you'd better consider how you feel about "Billy," because, like it or not, every child gets a nickname. You can't prevent nicknames, but you can try to avoid names you'd hate if abbreviated.

Names as (un)pleasant reminders

One of you may favor a name of a special friend as a way of honoring them. You might just as likely want to avoid certain names that would remind you of people you've been trying hard to forget. The names of old girlfriends or of guys who used to beat you up in school are not wise choices. Your lifelong best friend, on the other hand, would be a flattering and inspiring selection.

Family names

Many families pass on certain names out of tradition. Even if your families don't, you may want to honor a parent or relative whom you admire. The tricky part is that you and your partner both have families from which to choose names, and even if neither of you were planning to select a family name, you may discover that your families were hoping for or even expecting the courtesy.

GUY TALK

We had a boy's name picked out, but then it came out a girl. So we went with our ninth pick. It was tough finding a girl's name we both liked. I came up with ten choices that were acceptable to me and gave them to her and said, "Would you like our child to be named any of these?" And she said no. And she had ten names and I didn't like any of those. So it was really tough. Finally, I came up with Monique—a hot babe from the television show "Models, Inc."—and everybody liked it. And since I picked her first name, we used her mother's name as the middle name. That scored a lot of points.
—Kevin

If you find yourself being pressured, remember that you can't please everyone involved. The two most important people to satisfy are you and your partner. Go with a family name if that's really what the two of you want. If not, try to resist the pressure. Your relatives have already had their own opportunity to name their children. This is your first chance, and you deserve to make the final call.

"Guy Talk" tells what it was like for four guys trying to help name their baby. The clear moral we can draw from these stories is this: Guys are more likely to find a successful name from a babe-watch television show than from reading ancient historians. How would you like to suffer through Herodotus and still not get your choice of middle name?

The Rules

There are few rules to help you navigate the treacherous terrain of naming your child.

Your vote, as dad, counts more if your child is going to be a boy. Your partner gets the tie-breaker if it is a girl. Also, each partner has the generally accepted right to pass on their own first name to their same-sexed child. Finally, if you get to choose the first name, expect to concede the choice of middle name.

Beyond these basic guidelines, your final selection is likely to be a true test of your ability as a couple to give and take. Stand up for (or against) a name if you feel strongly. And, in an emergency case of prolonged baby-name debate, invoke the fear of the Unnamed Baby to bring your discussion to a timely conclusion.

In short, you can expect to discuss your baby's name sooner and more often than you can ever imagine this decision deserving.

Take comfort in knowing that Woodrow, Ronald, Lyndon, and Gerald are not just dorky names for boys, they're also the names of four former Presidents.

26 — FITTING IN AT THE BABY SHOWER

The '50s are over. That means you, a guy, could be invited to a baby shower.

I had always thought that baby showers were for women only. Imagine my surprise when my co-workers told me they were throwing me a baby shower. I was in a bit of a panic because I didn't know what I was being invited to, and I certainly wasn't going to *admit* it to any of them by asking. I was afraid I would be required to compete in party games I had never heard of. Would I be asked to make a speech? And why do they call them showers, anyway?

To spare you any unnecessary panic or concern, here is a simple primer that will help you conceal your ignorance about the baby-shower ritual:

The baby does not actually take a shower at a baby shower
Heck, the baby isn't even born yet. What happens at a baby shower is that your friends will "shower" your baby with gifts. Get it?

It's not what you get, it's how you react
Mothers-to-be have perfected their faked affection for baby-shower gifts by attending hundreds of other people's baby showers. You don't have that advantage. Fortunately, you can fake your way through with just two key phrases. Practice phrase #1 in front of a mirror until it sounds halfway believable when you say, "Oh, it's *sooo* cute!"

Repeat this phrase, over and over, after almost every gift you open. You'll think you're being redundant, but keep it up. Each person at the baby shower cares only about your reaction to *their* gift. They won't even realize you've said the magic phrase fifteen times already.

Every baby gift falls into one of two categories: cute or useful
You, as a guy, will undoubtedly receive things that you cannot identify or imagine how to use. So if it isn't cute, simply *assume* it's useful and repeat phrase #2: "Oh, it's *just* what we *need*!"

The advantage of this phrase is that you're probably right even though you don't know it yet. The female party guests will be impressed that you know the importance of their gift, and eventually you will discover its function.

Along with these two key phrases, there is one *banned phrase*. You must never, under any circumstance, open a gift and say, "We already have one."

You will probably get about three copies of *Goodnight Moon* (a great bedtime book—but you don't need to know that because you will simply say, "Oh, it's *just* what we *need*!"), lots of clothes ("They're *sooo* cute!"), and two baby monitors (pop-quiz time: cute or useful?). Just keep smiling. Your purpose at the shower is to let each gift-giver know that their present is valued.

If you don't get what you want, don't get glum. Here's a bonus baby-shower phrase for those duplicate gifts: "Wherever *did* you get this?!"

So don't fret over those bummer baby gifts. Find out where they came from. You'll return half of them later.

Perhaps your goal is to do more than merely *survive* the baby shower. If you desire to dazzle your female friends, you'll need to know much more about Official Baby Stuff.

OFFICIAL BABY STUFF:
YOU'VE NEVER HEARD OF IT BUT MUST HAVE IT

You might think starting a family is all about love, your commitment to your partner, and your desire to bring a new life into this world. Actually, having a baby is merely a means of fueling our nation's economy by draining your wallet.

Fortunately, your friends will give you many of the tools you'll need at baby showers. It will help you to know what you've been given so you can properly appreciate, and deploy, this arsenal of baby gear. Here are the most common and indispensable baby accessories.

Receiving Blanket

In case you wonder why they call them "receiving blankets," it's because you'll receive so many of them at baby showers. You may also wonder how to use them and why anyone would need more than one.

Just think of the receiving blanket as something you "receive" your child in. You lay, wrap, or—for advanced dads—"swaddle" your baby in the receiving blanket to keep it warm and to maximize its baby cuteness so you don't get frustrated by all that crying. Why more than one? You'll need lots of receiving blankets because your baby will tend to *throw up* on them.

Layette

A layette looks like a dress for babies. If you have a baby boy, I hope you're comfortable with his manhood, because this outfit is going to make him look like a sissy. But you won't care, because the design advantages of the layette far outweigh its girly looks. Basically,

GUY TALK

I wanted to know, "What's real and what's a rip-off? What do you really need?" Because I think, especially for women, there's a tendency to buy everything for the baby—because it's "for the baby!"
—Mike

a layette functions like pajamas but has a big opening at the bottom where the feet would normally be.

Why would anyone want a big opening in the bottom of their pants? As soon as your baby arrives, you'll see the obvious advantage, because you'll be changing between ten and twelve diapers a *day*. With a layette, you just hike that dress up, and you've got instant access. This feature may not excite you now, but wait until you change ten diapers in a day. You'll want to nominate the inventor for sainthood.

Aspirator

Remember how you faked your way through the baby shower by saying, "Oh, it's *just* what we *need!*" The aspirator is the ultimate example of something that (1) you'll have no idea what to do with and (2) you actually do need!

Babies have this nasty tendency to get "goo" in their throats. The aspirator is like a little air pump that you use to suction out your baby's mouth to prevent gagging. Aspirators will become your friend once you are properly introduced.

Baby Monitor

Baby monitors are a baby accessory every guy will love. Remember those cool battery-operated walkie-talkies we had when we were kids? Baby monitors work about the same way. You put a glorified microphone in the baby's room and put your baby "monitor" wherever you are, so you can leave the room and still be able to hear if anything goes wrong. These are delightful and expensive gifts.

In reality, you'll soon discover that nature has programmed you to be able to detect and overreact to the slightest twitch by your newborn, with or without the aid of high-tech monitors. But you'll want one because all the other parents will have them.

Diaper Genie

The Diaper Genie is the perfect answer to dreaded diaper odor. Why let diapers ripen in an ordinary garbage can when you can seal the smell inside this clever contraption? The Diaper Genie looks like an oversized thermos. You thrust dirty diapers through the opening on top and then, with a simple twist of the wrist, wrap the offender inside its own plastic bag. At the end of the week, simply empty the Genie and toss the contents into your garbage can. No mess, no stink!

I believe the Diaper Genie was invented by a brilliant woman who was frustrated by men's reluctance to help change diapers. She wisely knew men would gravitate to this high-tech toy. In the process, we get tricked into changing a few diapers.

While it may take you a while to figure out how to wedge the diapers into the Genie without sliming your hands, you will actually look forward to changing diapers because afterwards you can play with the Diaper Genie.

Changing Table

Sure, you know about diapers. Sure, you know about diaper disposals. But did you know you need a special table just for changing your baby? Changing tables aren't much to look at. A tool-type guy might logically hope for a few cool accessories, but a changing table is pretty much a table with a pad and railings on top to keep the baby from rolling off. But remember, there's nothing that says you can't soup up your changing table.

Once you've acquired all the necessary equipment for parenthood, you're ready to enter the home stretch.

Birthing class is about to begin. It's time to find out what a "kegel" is and whether you'd ever want to do one yourself.

part

SEVEN

7

HOME
STRETCH

28 BIRTHING CLASS

In the sixth month of pregnancy, you should plan to take a birthing class. Typically, these classes consist of six to eight sessions held once weekly on an evening or weekend. Usually an all-day crash course is also offered.

Even if you have been faithfully reading this book and attending the doctor's appointments, birthing classes are a great way to sharpen your knowledge before the big final exam.

Here are the top five benefits of attending birthing class:

1. You'll replace your fears with facts, and ignorance with information.
2. You'll learn specific techniques to help you through labor and delivery.
3. You'll build a strong coach-partner relationship with your partner.
4. You can bond with other expectant parents facing the same challenges, and you'll benefit from their support.
5. You'll get weekly opportunities to quiz an expert with your childbirth questions.

And here are five more reasons many guys enjoy birthing class:

1. You get a rare opportunity to safely commiserate with other guys about the joys of having a pregnant partner.
2. You have an excuse to get out of the house, which doesn't happen much at this stage of pregnancy.
3. You don't have to read *her* book as long as you pay attention in birthing class.

GUY TALK

We really enjoyed the every-week class thing. I learned a lot. By the end, we didn't want to leave the class. We really bonded with the other couples.
—Mike

4. You find good munchies, usually.
5. You see eye-opening films about childbirth.

Types of Birthing Classes

All birthing classes are designed to educate partners about the birthing experience and equip them with tools to minimize the pain of delivery. There are several types of birthing classes, each with its own philosophy about pain management and the use of drugs.

Here are four well-known approaches:

The Lamaze method
Lamaze teaches relaxation and breathing techniques that are synchronized to the expectant mother's contractions. You, as the dad, play the role of birthing "coach," helping your partner use the techniques. This method permits drugs if needed.

The Bradley method
Bradley allows normal breathing patterns and instead trains you, the dad, to distract your partner from pain by redirecting her focus toward different parts of her body. The Bradley method actively seeks to avoid any use of drugs.

The LeBoyer method
LeBoyer focuses on the experience of the baby rather than the mother. This approach emphasizes a more calm delivery-room atmosphere, immediate holding of baby by mom, and a delay in cutting the umbilical cord and other medical "interventions." This approach can be combined with either of the above methods.

The "Give-Me-Drugs" method
Drugs are widely understood by expectant moms. Oddly enough, many future moms are interested in using drugs to reduce the pain of childbirth.

Each birthing method takes a different view of the use of drugs during delivery, and each relies on a slightly different method of managing pain. Discuss with your partner how she would like the delivery to go and choose the class that best matches her wishes. Be prepared, however, to discover that your options are limited. In some communities and in some parts of the country, there may be only one approach taught in local birthing classes.

BY THE NUMBERS

Types of birthing class attended

Lamaze	69%
Bradley	9%
All other	22%

Your First Day at Birthing Class

Don't be surprised if your first reaction upon arriving at birthing class is to say to yourself, "I can't believe they are letting *these* people have children!" Don't worry. These people are probably thinking the same thing about you.

Odd as your group may initially appear, I predict that you will bond with them in ways that surprise you.

By the end of birthing class, these people will be your best friends. You will have shared your excitement and your fears. The impending birth experience often unites class members regardless of their backgrounds. It is a humbling reminder that parenting is something that everybody is allowed to do but nobody is ever completely qualified or prepared for.

Lights, Camera, Action!

A featured attraction at birthing class is the childbirth movie. You'll see childbirth in the hospital, at home, and in a tub. You'll see babies delivered in places you didn't realize they could be delivered.

You'll also hear *lots* of panting and screaming. This is a wake-up call. You may find that you have a whole new level of appreciation for what lies ahead. It's too late to turn back, so pay attention.

By the way, no refreshments are offered during these movies. The reason will be obvious once you've seen the first film.

The True Purpose of Birthing Class

The real point of birthing class is for you to learn your coaching role and for your partner to acquire a whole new set of terminology. Birthing classes will expose you to high doses of Prego Lingo. For example, what is a "kegel" exercise anyway, and why would anyone want to perform it?

Kegel exercises strengthen and tone a woman's pelvic muscles. The exercise involves contracting the pelvic muscles for five to ten seconds, starting with twenty-five and working up to as many as eighty repetitions.

Doing these exercises can prevent urinary incontinence, and toning these muscles can help both during delivery and in speeding a new mom's recovery.

There is a selfish reason for guys to be interested in this particular form of exercise. Kegels also enhance a woman's control of her vaginal muscles, an ability that can be used to heighten sexual pleasure. Kegels, anyone?

Male Bonding

Women are quick to share their feelings, hopes, and fears with their female friends. We guys are usually quicker with a sports score than a personal disclosure.

Consequently, one of the benefits for guys who attend birthing class is the chance to compare notes with other guys. During one of the many "potty breaks" that are necessary for the comfort and sanity of the expectant moms, seize the opportunity to do some male bonding.

The Big Picture

Having a baby is an experience that is simply too vast to digest in one day, week, or month. Birthing class helps you grasp the reality that, in just a few weeks, a rather large object will need to be pushed through a remarkably small opening in your partner's body, and it could hurt a lot and take a long time and put your partner in some danger. Birthing class gives you the knowledge you need in order to help her make it through with confidence and comfort. Well, at least with confidence.

BY THE NUMBERS

Attendance at birthing class

Yes, with husband	*70%*
Yes, with friend or family member	*5%*
No	*25%*

29 "GIVE ME DRUGS!"

Let's talk drugs. If men could be pregnant, we'd *all* want drugs during labor. But women really are the stronger sex. Miraculously, one-third of expectant moms have natural childbirth. For the rest, it is a simple decision: Pain is bad. Drugs relieve pain. So give me drugs!

But there is a virtual pharmacy to choose from: Spinal. Epidural. Narcotics. Local versus general. In addition, the drugs used during labor can make it harder to push the baby out and therefore might lengthen labor. Pregnant women often find themselves choosing between shorter labor but greater pain or less pain but longer labor.

Here's a pain-relief primer:

Analgesics
This group of pain-relieving drugs includes narcotic analgesics like Demerol. Non-narcotics include stronger doses of the familiar over-the-counter medicines like aspirin, ibuprofen (Advil, Nuprin), and acetaminophen (Tylenol). Analgesics are often administered intravenously, and they can prolong labor.

Regional or local anesthetics
These injections block pain sensations from a specific part of the body. The terms *regional* and *local* are often used interchangeably, though as you might expect, *regional* tends to refer to the numbing of a larger area of the body. The advantage of these injections is that the mother remains conscious. But depending on the exact location and the extent of the numbed area, they can also make pushing more difficult because she can't feel her pushing muscles. The most common types of injection are epidural, spinal, caudal,

GUY TALK

My wife definitely wanted drugs. She was asking for an epidural even before we conceived.
—John

or pudendal, and all refer to the numbing of specific areas of the body. See the glossary for more details.

General anesthetics

If needed at all, general anesthetics are most often used late in labor. This quick-acting anesthesia puts the patient to sleep and is generally reserved for emergency C-sections.

Fortunately, there is a simple rule of thumb when it comes to the decision about drugs during labor: Whatever she wants, she gets. *You* are not in pain, so butt out. This one is her decision.

BY THE NUMBERS

Use of drugs during labor

Epidural	48%
Narcotics	23%
Other	15%
None	37%

Many women head into their first delivery with noble intentions of natural childbirth. This is logical enough. After all, they've never actually experienced the pain of labor. But once reality sets in, relief from agony quickly becomes a focal concern.

What you can do is to be sure that you understand the risks, effects, and benefits of each of her pain-relief options. Your partner could possibly find herself in a situation where you might need to participate in the decision.

More likely, she'll know what she wants and when. Support her choices and encourage her to ask for what she needs. Many of us have a martyr streak inside, and there's no reason to let your mate suffer solely out of stubbornness. She might simply want your assurance that you won't think she's "wimping out" if she abandons her plan to have a natural birth. It's much more likely that she won't care one *bit* what you think of her, although she may share some choice opinions about what she thinks of *you*.

SCARY MOMENTS

It's normal to worry about your partner's health and your baby's health. This concern will be your companion throughout the pregnancy.

What you can't prepare yourself for, even though almost every couple experiences it, is the fear you feel when things suddenly aren't "normal."

This can be especially hard for guys, because we don't like to admit being scared. For instance, suppose you go skiing with your buddies. You come to the top of this really steep slope and you think to yourself, "I could *die* if I tried to ski that." But you don't want to be a wimp in front of your friends. Of course, each of them is thinking the same thing. What happens? *All* of you ski down this ridiculous precipice. At the bottom, you'll slap each other on the back and talk about how *awesome* that was, while secretly you are just glad to be alive. It's fun to be macho, as long as you live to tell about it.

But it's hard to stay macho throughout the nine months of pregnancy. At some point, almost every guy will be forced to face the fear that is inevitable when you are bringing a new life into the world.

In our case, my wife was diagnosed with pregnancy-induced high blood pressure and ordered onto immediate bed rest. There was a possibility, if it worsened, of real harm to her. Also, we were forced to face the likelihood of having to deliver our baby *very* early. The baby's lungs weren't fully developed yet, either. Then, a few weeks later, the doctors thought baby had stopped growing, so my wife was induced five weeks early. Our son weighed only three pounds at birth. I spent those last three weeks in constant fear for both mom and baby. I was a wreck.

GUY TALK

The baby hadn't moved in twenty-four hours. So she called me up at work and we rushed into the hospital to have some tests. They gave her some apple juice and the baby started jumping around and everything was OK. But it was one of those moments when I realize I understood more clearly—this was a life we were dealing with!
—Michael

*She was really
into* What to
Expect When . . . ,
*and when her symp-
toms didn't match
up, when she was
even missing one or
two—"I don't have
this right now"—
she'd want to call
the doctor. Actually,
she'd want to go to
the hospital! She'd
say, "I felt something"
or "I don't feel any-
thing"—which pretty
much covers 100
percent of the time!
—John*

*In the third
trimester she had
premature contrac-
tions that were very
scary for her. They
thought she was
going into labor at
six months. In the
middle of the day,
I got paged.
I returned the
page and it was
a call from the
hospital saying my
wife was having
contractions.
That was scary.
—John*

Even when it turns out that nothing is wrong, the slightest bump in the road to delivery can be unnerving. Here's what you need to know about pregnancy scares:

- Usually, these scares are just that—they are more frightening than they are dangerous. If you are *not* in real danger, the doctor will tell you.
- Even if the doctor tells you not to worry, you *will* worry, perhaps more deeply than ever before.

You've probably never felt more responsible for a life than you are now feeling for your child. It's an awesome and intimidating realization.

Part of what makes it hard is that there are so many things beyond your control. After all, there really is no such thing as an "average" pregnancy. The average pregnancy is a composite of a wide variety of experiences. When one part of your pregnancy doesn't coincide with the averages, it can be quite disturbing.

Fortunately, the actual rate of birth defects and problem pregnancies is remarkably low, thanks to terrific advances in medicine, early detection, and regular doctor visits. When anything unusual happens in your pregnancy, however, you are likely to experience it as a very real and present danger.

Your fear response isn't all bad. In the midst of this situation, you can reassure yourself that your fear is a measure of your concern and commitment as a parent-to-be. At the same time, you cannot afford to let your fears paralyze you. The best antidote for fear is facts.

If a complication does develop in your partner's pregnancy, put this book down. What you need to do is talk to your doctor, ask questions, and get informed.

Becoming informed won't necessarily make the problem go away, but it will help you know what the real risks are and whether there is anything you can do to help.

BY THE NUMBERS

Only 2 to 3 percent of babies are born with some type of birth defect.

You will be a bit busy, and maybe even a little tired and cranky, after your baby comes home. Here are a few conversations you should start before you actually become parents.

Breast-Feeding

Will your partner breast-feed your newborn? You might want her to breast-feed because you've read about the studies showing that breast milk enhances a baby's immune system. This is a sound reason for wanting to breast-feed, and research has strongly established the benefits of breast milk.

You might also want her to breast-feed because, let's face it, *you* don't want to have to get up in the middle of the night. This is not a good reason.

The question is, what to do with your opinions about breast-feeding? As with pregnancy in general, your vote counts less because you aren't the one who can carry out the decision. She's carrying the baby, and she'll be the one getting up in the middle of the night.

Many women choose on their own to breast-feed. If your partner is reluctant and you really feel strongly about the issue, offer to get one of those fancy electronic pumps so she can pump extra breast milk and bottle it. Then share the feedings—including late at night—using the bottled breast milk. An electronic breast pump can usually be rented on a monthly basis from the hospital where you're having your baby.

If you're not willing to share the work, you should respect her choice if she's not comfortable breast-feeding.

The other possible scenario that can cause friction is when your partner *does* want to breast-feed. Some guys are concerned that they will be "left out" and miss the special bonding experience that seems to go hand in hand with feeding a newborn.

Again, the pump-and-share approach is an excellent compromise. Most women would be delighted if their partners begged to share the feeding chores—especially that 2 a.m. shift.

The First Weeks

After the baby is born, how much time will you take off work to be with and care for your child—and to help mom recuperate?

Many states offer parental-leave programs that permit both partners to stay home for as many as twelve weeks after the birth of a baby. Some or all of this time off may be paid. Check with your employer for their specific policy.

Your choice may be influenced not only by your personal finances and your company's family-leave policy but also by company politics. Do other men at your company take time off when they become dads? How much time do they take?

Parental leave for dads is one area where men may find they are expected to conform to the old rules and "put the job first" rather than taking time off.

I knew that other guys where I worked took only a few weeks off. But I really wanted to spend more time with my baby than that. Also, I had the feeling that I could help raise the bar to make it OK for other guys at the office to take off the amount of time they wanted. So I took four weeks off and worked part-time for another four. Afterwards, several other expectant dads thanked me for making it easier for them to ask for time off. This is a tough decision that only you can make. But you may want to fall back on the old "ten year" axiom: "Ten years from now, which will have been a more important way to spend this time—at home or at the office?"

Along with work pressures, you may also feel pressure on the home front to take time off. And why not? Think of how your partner's body has been taken over for the past nine *months*. After delivery, she will be understandably exhausted—*and* responsible for this tiny new life. She needs you at home as much as the baby does.

In addition, these early weeks offer a unique bonding opportunity between you and your new child. It's hard to imagine regretting spending extra time with your newborn.

There are compelling reasons to take as much time off as your job and income permit. At the same time, the pressure to get back to work is real. In addition, not everyone discovers that they enjoy, or are good at, parenting an infant. Many new parents report—with understandable guilt—how eager they were to return to the relatively easy job of working at the office, compared to the challenge of parenting a newborn. It's OK to admit you need a work break to be a better parent when you *are* home.

The best thing you can do is discuss your parenting goals and your time-off fears with your partner in advance so that you can jointly generate a plan that takes care of baby, mom, dad, and your family's finances.

Childcare

Who will care for your baby after those first few weeks? Do you want your partner to stay home? Does she? Can you both afford this option? If not, what kind of childcare environment do you want and can you afford? These are tough questions, and you'd better begin to struggle with them before your child is born.

At the same time, remember that you can't really know what parenting *feels* like until your baby arrives. You might hope to be a stay-at-home dad, working in a home office, only to discover that you were kidding yourself about getting work done at home while parenting a newborn. Or your partner might want to be a full-time mom yet realize that she's a better parent if she gets a break half the time.

I was the one in our household who was more interested in being the stay-at-home parent. After our son was born, I quickly learned two things. First, I was dreaming to think I could be a productive worker from home and also be a good parent. Second, I was forced to admit that I wasn't a very patient full-time parent. I did a much better job of parenting when I was gone at the office for part of the day than when I was home full-time.

You can't know in advance how you'll respond to the rewards and challenges of parenthood. Still, this is a great time to research your options. For example, call childcare centers early. Many of the best have waiting lists. Also, talk to friends who are recent parents and interview them about their experiences, choices, and level of satisfaction.

If at all possible, explore these options without committing yourself to one decision. Many expectant parents find out parenting wasn't what they expected. For some it was more rewarding, and for others, more difficult. So give yourself the chance to discover, after birth, what will work best for your entire family.

32   TO BEEP OR NOT TO BEEP

As you close in on the Big Day, you may begin to worry, What if my partner delivers unexpectedly and I can't be reached? Fear of missing the birth is natural. And if *you* don't worry about it, you can be sure that your partner will.

In today's increasingly connected world, the chances of you being out of touch when the moment finally arrives are fairly slim. People now climb Mount Everest and phone home from the summit to let everybody know they made it. Beepers are becoming as essential as bookbags for today's high school kids, and let's not even get started on the whole global-village Internet frenzy. Still, you need to pick from the wide array of possibilities available to make sure you have a foolproof way of being reached. If you already have a cell phone, that may be all you need. If you've been wanting a cell phone, now may be your best opportunity to convince your partner that you need one. The simplest and most affordable option is a beeper. Most delivering hospitals now offer short-term beeper rentals to expectant dads. The things are tiny these days and don't even necessarily have to beep. You can set it to vibrate and you won't get dirty looks when it goes off in the movie theater.

Whatever method you choose, you may start to feel an increased sense of self-importance. After all, people look at somebody with a beeper and think, "Wow that guy must be really important." Or they say to themselves, "That guy must be a drug dealer and if I'm not careful he could have me killed." Either way you get a little extra respect. The downside, of course, is that you are always available. When your partner calls, you have to answer.

GUY TALK

I wanted the beeper. We rented one from the hospital for the month. It was a pretty good deal. I was glad I had it. I was excited. I didn't want to miss out! I was going to be there, regardless.
—Mike

When she tries to reach you, either she's having the baby or she's not. Once the novelty of being a big shot wears off, you will learn to fear *both* scenarios.

Let's say you are actually doing something important for a change. She calls. Your heart races and you drop your project, breathless:

You: Is it time?
Her: Time for what?
You: To go to the hospital!
Her: Oh, *no*, silly. I just called to see what you were doing…
You: I was *working*. Is that what you called me to ask?
Her: What, don't you want to talk to me?

Before you know it, you've been duped by another Trick Question and you're trapped in a "Don't you love me?" conversation when in fact you are the innocent victim of a test of the Emergency Delivery System. (If this were a real delivery, you would be instructed to drive to the hospital.)

Before you get mad and turn off the pager or quit answering your phone, let your partner know how you feel about non-urgent calls. Or, if you think about the real reason she's calling, you may decide to just play along. After all, late in the pregnancy, many women have a greater need for closeness and connection. She may feel more isolated, and it may be comforting to know you are there for her when she really needs to just talk and say "hi."

Of course, sooner or later you will be called for the Real Thing. This obvious fact will somehow be forgotten the moment you receive that fateful call. "*What!*" responds the typical guy. "You're having the *baby*? Right now?"—as though this is some big surprise. After nine months of preparation and waiting, it's time for action.

GUY TALK

They'll beep you for absolutely no good reason. They'll just be testing. I'd get beeped twice a day. I had the beeper and she knew it was on me, so it became this ball-and-chain thing!
—John

8

DELIVERY
DAY

Getting ready to go to the hospital is like preparing for the ultimate backwoods camping trip. You could bring everything you own and still feel inadequately prepared.

While you can't ever be sure of everything you'll need, there are some basics that should be in your bag and on your list.

Oh, and by the way, pack the bag ahead of time. This is Baby Room Frenzy all over again. Your partner may want to pack this bag the day after the pregnancy test comes back. You can probably eke out a few extra months, but if you are still contemplating the perfect packing job during the week that she's due, prepare for a fight!

Here's what you should pack:

Comfort items for her
- Favorite music (if she finds it relaxing)
- Sugarless suckers (her mouth will get dry)
- Socks (to keep her feet warm)
- Oils or lotions (for massaging her back and body)
- Washcloth and hairbrush (for comfort-cooling and grooming)
- Favorite perfume
- Toiletries, robe, and extra clothes for going home
- Her pregnancy book

Stuff for you
- Stopwatch or clock (for timing contractions, coach)
- Snacks/sandwiches (they'll take care of feeding her)
- Cards, a game, or magazines to entertain you both

GIRL TALK

He just refused to pack the bag until the day before we went to the hospital. What's the problem? It only took ten minutes to pack the bag! And he insisted on doing it, but he just kept putting it off. I think it was his way of denying the reality of, yes, we are really having a baby!
—Carrie

- Your favorite pillow (it could be a long night)
- Still or video camera (see chapter 35 before you shoot)
- A gift (see chapter 37)
- This book, if you haven't already committed it to memory

Things for the baby
- His/her first outfit
- His/her first toy

Even though the little fellow might have no idea that the rattle is even there, *you* will get a thrill out of it, so knock yourself out.

Before you finalize your list and your bag, check with the hospital where you'll be delivering. Every facility offers different services. For example, your hospital may have a fridge stocked just for expectant dads. So compare your list with services offered by your hospital before you over- (or under-) pack.

There are also a few things you should *not* take to the hospital:

- Your laptop ("Just gonna do a *little* work, honey")
- Videos of past Super Bowl games
- A Walkman, if your intent is to drown her out
- Your cell phone, unless it's to call relatives with the big news
- Two or three new books ("Thought I'd catch up on my reading")

Congratulations. Your bags are properly packed. You're settled into your room. But you still have this one nagging question in your mind: Will I faint?

$\mathcal{34}$ WILL I FAINT?

Every normal guy asks himself this question: Will I pass out during delivery?

First of all, take comfort in knowing that your fears are normal. Most guys worry about fainting. And here's more good news. Hardly anybody actually faints.

The best way to increase your odds of staying vertical is to learn about the delivery process.

Attending childbirth classes will give you much of the information you need to replace your fears with confidence.

Or, if you missed the flicks at your childbirth classes, you could rent one of the many videos that show actual childbirth. Watching a video will give you a valuable preview of your own delivery.

It also helps to "know thyself." Some guys can watch heart surgery on the Discovery Channel and eat dinner at the same time. Other men whimper like babies at the sight of their own blood.

If you have a naturally queasy stomach, plan on looking elsewhere during the more graphic moments of delivery. Just be prepared to surprise yourself. When it comes to your child entering the world, you'll be amazed at how interested you can be, despite your fears.

Also, be sure to take time out to regularly refuel. In your efforts to take care of your partner's every need, you may forget to take care of yourself. Eating at regular intervals will help ensure that you stay on your feet.

Take comfort in knowing that your fears are natural. If you stay focused on your fears, you may have problems. More likely, you'll focus on your partner and on what you can do to support her. If you are engaged and focused on what's happening in the moment, you'll find

GUY TALK

When they gave my wife the epidural, it was tough. I couldn't see anything, but the anesthesiologist's description made me queasy. I had to kneel down, and then I felt better.
—Paul

that there is far too much interesting stuff going on for you to have time to think about fainting.

Missing the Birth, Part Two

Most men worry about fainting and missing the birth of their child. Few consider the possibility that they might be kept out of the delivery room, but it does sometimes happen.

For example, some hospitals don't allow dads to be present during C-sections. Find out in advance if there are any situations at your hospital where you would be excluded from the delivery room. If you learn about any conflicts in policy ahead of time, you can prepare options.

The odds are, however, that if you *want* to be present at the birth, you will be.

Since you plan to be in the delivery room and on your feet, let's talk about what you can do to make yourself *useful*.

GUY TALK

I don't know any guy who hasn't worried about fainting. I certainly was. You're afraid that, at the crucial moment, you won't be there for your one job she's counting on you to do.
—Paul

LIGHTS, CAMERA...DELIVERY!

"And ... action!"

Using a video camera is one of the few tasks during pregnancy that we guys are trained to handle. Taking videos enables us to use our natural affinity for high-tech toys while doing something useful for our partner at the same time.

After all, what woman wouldn't want to preserve on film forever that special moment of the birth of her child?

Answer? Lots.

This is important information for you, as a dad-to-be, to know in advance. Otherwise, the "special moment" you capture on film will be your enraged partner screaming, "You shut that thing off right *now* or *else*."

This is not the kind of special moment you were intending to preserve for posterity. It may become very funny to you years later. Your partner, on the other hand, might never find any humor in it.

So the question you must ask yourself is: To film, or not to film? The only sane approach is to ask your partner ahead of time. If you *want* to film the birth, think about your reasons. Let your partner know what you hope to capture and why—and then ask her how she feels about it.

Most women, quite naturally, will be reluctant to have the most painful moment of their entire life captured forever on film. They feel very large, very unattractive, and very uncomfortable. Imagine feeling that way about yourself and having your partner ask to videotape *you*.

Even with all this self-consciousness, moms-to-be recognize the specialness of this moment, and most

GUY TALK

Oh yeah, I filmed it. Kept it clean. She kind of wanted it, and I said, "Who's gonna see this video, anyway?"
—Kevin

We had a party to watch our video— with thirty people there!
—Mike

are open to some kind of "record." Be flexible and creative. If your partner doesn't want the delivery itself taped, offer to stop recording at a specific point in the process. Let her know she can ask you to stop at any time, but don't put the burden of doing so on her. She's already a bit busy.

Another less-threatening option is to take photographs. Again, find out in advance from your partner where the no-more-pictures point is and honor it, despite the temptation.

Most importantly, remember that your primary duty in the delivery room is not "documentary director." Do what you can to capture the moments, but make sure your primary focus is on supporting your partner and helping her every way you can. Despite what some people claim, focusing a camera is easier than delivering a baby.

36 | THE DELIVERY

For nine months, you've both been wishing this day would hurry up and arrive. Now she's in labor and you wish you had more time to prepare, because you aren't ready yet!

Before the labor progresses too far, you should make doubly sure you're clear on your role during labor and delivery. Also, you and your partner should establish any ground rules in advance for who else will be part of your birthing experience.

Ground Rules

Who do you want to be present? When? Do you want part of the delivery to be shared by only you and your partner? When can relatives see the baby?

These issues are awkward to resolve once labor has begun. Your mind will be on more pressing matters. Consult with your mate ahead of time and let your relatives know what you've decided, even if you think they might be upset. Better to be honest about what you want, in advance, than to have your birth experience compromised or to get in a delivery-room argument.

BY THE NUMBERS

Who's with mom in the delivery room

Baby's father	96%
Other family members	27%
Friend(s)	11%

GUY TALK

At the birth of our first, I was hurt because the mother-in-law just forgot about me. She was holding the baby a lot and hovering over me when I held her. I understand her feelings—but give me five minutes with my own child, give me my space. So with our second, we got everybody out just before the delivery.
—Kevin

DELIVERY STAGES

	Early Labor	Active Labor	Transitional Labor	Delivery	After Birth
AVERAGE LENGTH	Several hours to a day or more	2½ to 6 hours	Brief to 2 hours	30 minutes to 3 hours	5 minutes to 1 hour
DILATION	3 cm.	From 3 cm. to 8 cm.	From 8 cm. to 10 cm.	Completely dilated	
CONTRACTIONS	30 to 45 seconds long, 5 to 20 minutes apart	40 to 60 seconds long, 3 to 4 minutes apart	Intense, 60 to 90 seconds long, 2 to 3 minutes apart	60 to 90 seconds long, farther apart (2 to 5 minutes)	
HER EXPERIENCE	• Longest but least painful phase • Symptoms may include cramps, backaches, indigestion, and diarrhea	• Backaches likely • Harder to relax • Contractions harder • Less conversational	• Most difficult phase for her • May "tune you out" because of pain and focus	• Pushing phase • Hard, active work	• Relieved • Energized or exhausted • Thirsty!
WHAT YOU CAN DO	• Practice timing contractions • Keep her occupied with conversation, games, and humor • Take care of yourself, too: Eat	• Coach her with breathing • Keep the room calm (lower lights, play music) • Use your comfort props (washcloth, ice chips, warm socks, etc.) • Give her backrubs	• Continue relaxation techniques • Help her take contractions one at a time, then relax between • Take your cues from her re touching and talking • Give her lots of encouragement	• Coach her pushing and breathing • Encourage her with progress reports • Take your cues from her	• Congratulate her! • Help her with fluids • Hold the baby!

Your Role During Delivery

You are the coach. She is the quarterback. The hard part about being the coach, as guys well know, is that the quarterback is really the one who has to go out and get the job done. Your role is vitally important, and few quarterbacks could succeed without a good coach behind them. The quarterback, however, is in control.

That doesn't mean you should fall into the role of bystander. Labor and delivery lasts as long as *four* football games—including time-outs for commercials—and even the best "quarterbacks" need to lean on their coach for support and guidance. Keep asking and thinking about what you can do to help your partner. To be a good coach, in labor as well as in sports, you must keep your head in the game, constantly looking for ways to help your "quarterback" succeed.

You Don't Have to Be Perfect

Give yourself permission to make mistakes as coach. In the excitement of the moment, you may not remember everything you learned in birthing class. In fact, you may realize you've done something *wrong*. During delivery, being perfect is less important than being *present*. You are *expected* to be clueless, which is why the *doctor* is there. Focus on what you can do now and what you can do next.

Also, be prepared for her to tell you to "lay off" for a while. Sometimes the best help you can give her is to let her work through a tough spot on her own. Every delivery is different, and every couple relates differently.

Several times during our delivery, my wife found my efforts at support distracting, and she was not reluctant to tell me so. I backed off. After a while, I asked again and she was ready for more help.

BY THE NUMBERS

Did pregnant women use birthing-class lessons at birth?

Yes	67%
No	33%

She Doesn't Mean What She Says

Some guys would consider themselves lucky if all their partner said to them was "Back off." Labor and delivery will probably be the most intense experience of your partner's life. And you did have something to do with her present predicament. Consequently, she may hurl a few not-so-carefully-chosen words your way during delivery.

Decide in advance to forgive anything she might say once you arrive at the hospital. Sure, she might *sound* like she means it. In that moment, she probably does. But it's your duty to keep it all in perspective. You can always blame her epithets on the drugs.

Fortunately for her and for you, the pain will pass. She may not even remember saying some of the things that *you* know she said. There's no need to play back that secret audio recording you made. Just be glad she can't remember, because if she really did mean it, she might not forget so quickly.

What She Needs and When

The average length of labor for a first-time mom is around twelve hours. Within labor and delivery, there is a series of stages. You know this because you paid attention in birthing class. You also need to remember, though, that few births ever go exactly by the book.

You should keep this book open to the table on the previous page the entire time you're at the hospital. This table outlines what she will most likely be experiencing, and what you can do, at each stage during delivery.

This is only a reference. Your partner's body has the final say, so listen to her first and use this as a reference for what you can try at each stage to help coach her through labor and delivery.

As coach, it is helpful for you to know what's "normal." But—like the announcer says in those car commercials—actual results may vary. The most important thing you can do as coach is to stay focused on your partner's needs and her particular delivery experience, whether normal or not.

Seeing Your Baby

This is the moment you've been looking forward to for nine months. There's no right or wrong thing to do or way to react. Take your time and savor the moment.

You might even put down your camera. This is an image you'll be able to preserve in your mind forever.

GIRL TALK

He was very supportive. Just being there, holding my hand, asking if there was anything I wanted, feeding me ice chips . . .
—Janice

37 THE GIFT

Your newborn child is perhaps the most wonderful gift you will receive in your life. But this chapter is *not* about *that* gift.

What we're talking about here is the gift you buy your partner—in *advance*—and present to her on the occasion of the birth of your child. (Pause here while thousands of men everywhere gasp in shock.)

If this book were written solely from the point of view of men, this chapter would not exist. Guys barely remember gifts at Christmas and birthdays. Our brains are not wired to think in terms of "gifts" for things like this. After all, we helped out at the delivery, didn't we? What more does a woman want?

When I asked women what one thing expectant dads needed to know, they were unanimous about the need for some kind of acknowledgment for their nine months of carrying and delivering your child. Believe me, I tried to talk them out of this idea.

Read "Girl Talk" to see what some of them had to say.

Now you know what you're up against. My theory is that some guy, somewhere, gave *his* wife jewelry. Before the day was over, she had informed pregnant women *everywhere*, and since then, each of them has taken personal responsibility for continuing to spread the word to all other women. So now we guys have to pay!

As you can tell from the comments of these women, the process of buying and giving this gift isn't a simple one. If you want to get credit for getting her a gift, you'll need to be clear on the rules pregnant women have for The Gift:

We have just delivered your baby through our body. Do you think that this maybe deserves a little recognition? A card, maybe? How about a gift! Let's see. The guy works for nine minutes, the woman works for nine months. Hmm. A present is in order. In recognition for what your wife has just presented you— the biggest gift of all time—which you can never duplicate!— a gift, please!
—Janice

A reward? Oh yeah! Of course! Just a little . . . something! Pregnancy is something guys can't do! I did expect something. Where was my bouquet? He did give me some flowers, but I thought he might have got them from the room next door. You do kind of expect that, after nine months, you'll get something!
—Carrie

It should be big
After all, she is comparing this gift to her gift to you— nine months of physical and emotional sacrifice culminating in the childbirth experience.

Jewelry is the gift of choice among the women I polled. Flowers and an elegant dinner (*not* pizza) earned honorable mention.

If you buy jewelry, you must get actual jewelry
Jewelry, according to women, refers to earrings, a necklace, a watch, or a bracelet. These items are not to be confused with *accessories*, like a broach or a pin, which will actually result in your *losing* rather than scoring points.

You must buy your gift in advance
She figures that you've had nine months to anticipate this moment. If you wait to run down to the hospital gift shop, she'll likely be hurt that you treated it as an afterthought. Unless, of course, it's a *big* piece of jewelry.

Of course, women say they want jewelry. But you know what? I'm pretty sure anything you do will be a big hit as long as you've put thought into it and it expresses your acknowledgment and appreciation for what she's done these past nine months.

9 GOING HOME

38

THE FIRST WEEK

Congratulations. You have survived nine months of pregnancy, and you have a wonderful little baby to show for your efforts. You've brought the baby home. You're done.

Guys naturally see the delivery as the end point, the culmination and completion of this nine-month journey. It might seem strange to you if your partner doesn't share your enthusiasm.

You are excited. You are proud. You are not bleeding internally.

Delivery marks the end of pregnancy, but the effects of those nine months do not evaporate overnight. Your partner will continue to display symptoms of the Pregnancy Zone for several more weeks. Here's what is likely to happen to your partner's body in the first days and weeks after birth:

Bleeding
Especially in the first few days, she will probably experience bloody discharges. Over the course of the first two weeks, these will slowly dissipate.

Nature calls
She's been through a lot. Nothing else is going to come out of her unless it is absolutely necessary. She may be constipated for the entire first week! How comfortable do you think *that* will be?

Pain
Her body will probably feel like a human punching bag, complete with aches, soreness, and cramping. Do I need to remind you *why* she's sore?

Breasts
Big? Yes. Painful. *Yes!* Her breasts, which swell with milk for the baby, can feel quite painful until her body finds that natural balance where it produces the same amount of milk as the baby consumes.

Breast-feeding

This might seem natural to guys. But the actual technique of breast-feeding is difficult for baby and painful for mother. Her nipples will probably be very sore for a while.

Weight loss

An average-sized woman will gain twenty-five to thirty-five pounds during pregnancy. Your partner will probably be impatient to have her old body back. Until she sees signs of her former figure returning, this can be a source of anxiety and frustration for her. You also may be anxious about whether she'll recapture her former size, but this is probably not a good time to verbalize those fears.

You can help by participating with her in moderate exercise and by reassuring her that she looks good to you just the way she is—even if you're not sure you feel that way!

GIRL TALK

On the second day, my husband invited the neighbors over. He was so excited, it was sweet. He wanted to show her off. But guys, before you invite people over, check with your wife. You're not as tired, you're not in as much pain, you don't have the bleeding thing going on. If she tells you to lie and say that the baby's sleeping, lie and say, "The baby's sleeping!"
—Janice

BY THE NUMBERS

In one study of pregnant women, only 28 percent had returned to their pre-pregnancy weight by the sixth to eighth week after delivery.

No-no's

There are several ways you can unintentionally get yourself into big trouble in the first week:

Tell anyone who'll listen what a "wonderful moment" the birth was
You deserve to be excited about becoming a dad. At the same time, try to be sensitive to the fact that—at that same moment of birth—someone else was working *really hard* and may not have had the same opportunity to see and enjoy the "moment."

Invite your entire office and every living relative to come visit and see your new baby child
You are the proud pappa. You want to show off. Of course you do. *Your* body hasn't been ravaged by

pregnancy. You don't have an infant nursing at your breast every two hours. You may even be getting a little sleep at night.

Meanwhile, your partner probably still cares how she looks and how the house looks, just like she always has. The difference is, during the first week after the baby comes home, she has neither the energy nor the time to do much about either. She may be a remarkable woman who doesn't care and says, "Sure, invite them over." More likely, she does care and would prefer to have guests in smaller doses and at times when she's feeling up to the task. Always ask her first *before* inviting people on baby tours.

Talk about what a great night's sleep you had

This is a good way to ensure that it will be your last good night's sleep.

If your partner is breast-feeding, you might consider offering to get the baby up at night and change its diaper before handing the baby off to her for the night feeding. It will give your mate a little more sleep and give you a little more empathy, not to mention a genuine sense of involvement and partnership in your baby's care.

At a minimum, don't brag. Your partner would love to be able to sleep through the night. Nature has assigned her a role that prevents this simple pleasure. If she truly doesn't mind handling the night-feeding chores, let her know how much you appreciate her efforts and ask what you can do in some other part of the day to help *her*.

There's another self-interested reason why you should pitch in more in those first few weeks. You have a lot of making up to do if you hope to ever touch her again!

39

SEX AGAIN!

"How long do I have to wait?"

This is the question that many guys begin asking themselves—and sometimes their partner—approximately two minutes after their child is born. Never mind the fact that, an hour ago, she may have said, "Touch me again, *ever*, and *I'll kill you.*" Being a guy, you've already forgotten and have moved on to, well, your own selfish needs.

Time for a reality check!

When it comes to resuming romantic relations, guys are often like a caged bull, pawing at the ground, eager to charge into action the moment it is released from its pen.

Don't be surprised if your partner is less enthused. In addition, you might discover that *you* are the one who is cautious.

For some guys, the sight of a baby coming out of their partner's body changes the way they see her. She may now seem more like a remarkable birthing machine than a tempting seductress. This is both normal and temporary. As her body recovers and reshapes, most men find that their sexual fires reignite.

You may also find that it's hard to be "in the mood" for love when you're really in the mood for a nap. Most parents of newborns spend a lot of time fantasizing about being in bed. But their fantasy is to be *asleep* in bed.

More often, though, guys are ready to go while mom is still reeling from the physical trauma of pregnancy and childbirth.

Imagine things from her point of view. She has a life that is completely dependent on her and demands her constant attention. And now she has a new baby, too!

In addition, her body is bruised and sore. Her breasts ache from being so full of baby's milk. She very likely does

GIRL TALK

Everyone wants something from you. The baby, your husband, your friends. Give us a chance to recover! We're exhausted and our body hurts a lot.
—*Nancy*

not *feel* attractive because her body is still stretched and puffy. So how romantic do you think she feels?

The rule of thumb is to wait six weeks. This is just a general guideline. If you pounce on your partner six weeks to the day, be prepared for rejection. Every woman's body and every woman's sexual appetite recover at different rates. Talk about your desires for intimacy, let your partner know you find her attractive, and take it slow.

While you await the green light—whether your own or hers—consider some "baby steps" toward intimacy. Since you're both going to be fatigued from caring for your newborn, you would do well to cultivate simpler ways of caring for each other.

Remember how much she appreciated those back-rubs or foot-rubs during pregnancy? Guess what? She will *still* enjoy a massage even though the baby has been delivered. Massage can be a wonderful way to gently enjoy each other's body.

You could also plan a dinner by candlelight or rent a movie and try some good old-fashioned snuggling. Cuddling lets her know you still love her while being tender toward her body. She'll appreciate that you both desire and respect her.

When you do receive the green light, be prepared for the possibility of different sensations and different rules. Your partner's body has changed, so expect it to feel different to you.

Here's one final point to ponder before you leap back into romance: Remember where this led last time? Before you go charging back to bed, you'd better discuss whether you want to have more kids.

BY THE NUMBERS

Length of time women say it took to regain their pre-pregnancy desires

Less than 3 months	62%
3–5 months	9%
6–9 months	7%
More than 9 months	22%

40   HAVING MORE KIDS

It's hard to imagine having more kids—or even talking about it—when you've barely left the hospital.

On the other hand, the whole "having kids" thing has been pretty much the *only* thing on your mind for the past few weeks. So don't be surprised if you wind up discussing the question shortly after your baby is born.

You might think it is premature to discuss having another child when you have not even tried parenting the first. That's a sensible observation. But it won't prevent you from asking the inevitable question, "Would we ever do this again?"

For months, your life together has been focused almost solely on the process of having a child. In fact, by now you've probably driven all your single friends away with your detailed accounts of each stage of pregnancy.

Nevertheless, the intensity of this experience can bring couples much closer together. These intense feelings, in all of their extremes from love and joy to anxiety and fear, can leave you wanting more.

So it's quite natural that you would discuss—right after the birth—whether either of you would ever want to go through this experience again.

There are three basic options: Have another child, delay deciding, or never have another baby.

A typical "more kids" conversation might start with her saying, "You will never touch me again!" This could be a hint that you might *not* be having more kids.

Having a child, as you now finally understand, is a *big deal*. So whoever does *not* want another child gets a bigger vote. Suppose you want another child. If she does, too, great. If not, *she* gets the tie-breaker. If she wants a child and *you* don't, you should both wait.

While you probably can't resist discussing the issue, I encourage you not to *decide* yet. You might want to discover a little more about what *parenthood* is like before you commit!

If and when you arrive at option three—no more kids—be prepared for the inevitable question: How are we going to make *sure*?

At this point, I can virtually guarantee that you will find yourself discussing a certain kind of surgery related to an important part of the male anatomy.

"You Want Me to What?"

Can you say "vasectomy"? I assure you that your partner can. If you've just had your last child, get ready for her to ask *you* to be the one to decommission your baby-making gear.

She's got you. After all, she just carried your baby inside her body for nine months. In the corporate world, this is what is called a strong bargaining position.

Are you really going to try to argue that (1) it might hurt and (2) she should be the one, instead of you?

I don't think so. What's worse, if you go ahead and get the big "V," you can't *complain* about the discomfort, or you'll just be inviting her to remind you of the Golden Rule of Expectant Dads: "It could be worse— *you* could have been pregnant."

EPILOGUE

Congratulations. You have emerged from the clutches of the Pregnancy Zone. Your reward is the most precious of all gifts—a newborn child.

Of course, the ending of pregnancy instantly turns into the beginning of parenthood. You may be too stunned by the demands of your new role to appreciate what you've just accomplished.

In addition, you may have come to the sobering realization that pregnancy lasts only nine months, whereas you'll be in the Parenthood Zone for life.

In case you're either dazed or distressed—or both—take a moment to reflect on what you've accomplished. As you begin to face the challenges of parenthood, your achievements during these past nine months can be a source of strength:

- You've learned to identify and disarm her trickiest questions, and as a result, your mate is still speaking to you.
- The baby has a room. The room is fully furnished, even if it was close.
- You've kept the romance alive in your relationship despite the changes in your partner's body and in each of your moods.
- You've overcome the guy urge to "do" by learning to play a supportive role.
- You've managed to synchronize her timing ("now") with yours ("later").
- In labor, you faced your fears and found new strength in partnership with your mate. Now you have a wonderful little baby.
- As a bonus, you are passably fluent in Prego Lingo and can fake your way through a baby shower, in case you're ever invited to one again.

As you immerse yourself in the world of parenting, remember the lessons you've learned. Trick Questions will continue to appear. You'll definitely still need Boys' Night Out now that you're a parent. Romance also continues to require more effort with a baby in the house.

Caring for Each of Your Roles

You've always had a duty to take care of yourself and your partner. Now you've added a new role: Dad.

You'll be a great dad if you remember the active role you played in your partner's pregnancy. Take the same approach to caring for your newborn child. This is not just mom's job, and you'll be richly rewarded for the time you invest.

You also must remember to take care of yourself as parenthood increases the demands on your time and energy. Continue to communicate with your mate to find a workable way you can enjoy activities that meet your personal needs.

Finally, you will need to make a special effort to nourish your relationship with your mate. Your child will consume much of the time you used to spend focused on each other. Remember the creative ways you found to keep romance alive while your partner kept expanding. Consider scheduling a regular "date night" without kids. The best way to be good parents is to take good care of each other first.

During your nine months in the Pregnancy Zone, you experienced great joys and scary moments, and hopefully you can look back with a sense of being both stronger and wiser for the journey.

At a minimum, the Golden Rule of Expectant Dads remains true: "It could be worse—*you* could have been pregnant."

PROFILES

These are the people behind the stories. I thank them for their candor about their pregnancy experiences.

Mike is a self-employed marketing consultant. As a new dad, he appreciates the help he's received along the way from his own parents and his in-laws, too. He and his wife, Carrie, have each been married before, and they have a baby girl together.

Kevin has worked at the same manufacturing plant for more than fifteen years. He comes from a large family, and so far he and his wife have two children: a girl and a boy. If Kevin gets his way, more kids will follow!

Paul is a researcher for a nonprofit civic organization. He and his wife have a baby girl, and he looks back on his pregnancy experience as full of life lessons.

John is a radio and television personality. He was divorced and has remarried, and now he has a toddler. He considers a sense of humor vital to surviving the nine months of pregnancy, and he has lots of stories to prove it.

Michael is a salesman. He found out he was going to be a dad on his birthday. He is introspective about pregnancy and parenthood, and his biggest concern is that he be a good father. He and his wife have one child.

Janice works part-time as a television producer. She thinks men need to be more sensitive to their pregnant partner's needs and she gladly spells out exactly what men should and should not do. She and her husband have two children: a little girl and a baby boy.

Nancy is a sales manager who's not shy about telling her partner how she feels. She values her career and likes to dress professionally even when pregnant, and she doesn't feel guilty about either. She and her husband have two children.

Carrie is Mike's wife. She works for a company that markets labels for wine bottles. She thought she was the perfect pregnant partner—until she overheard Mike talking on the phone to one of his buddies.

ACKNOWLEDGMENTS

This book would not have been possible without the many men and women who shared with me their pregnancy experiences. This nine-month journey elicits every possible emotion from fear to elation, and I am indebted to each one of these parents for their openness and their honesty that inspired and informed this book.

In addition, I would like to thank Jennifer Lauck, for believing in me as a writer and urging me to dare to write a book; to Carrie and Mike, for suggesting this idea and saying, "You should write a *book* about that!"; Lisa Schneiderman, who encouraged me in this project and connected me with the great staff at Beyond Words Publishing; Cindy Black and Kathy Matthews at Beyond Words, for seeing the value in a book that seeks to help men be better pregnancy partners and for their tireless efforts to create the best possible book; my agent, Nancy Love, for her patient and thorough explanations of the business of publishing and her efforts representing me; and Lois Randall, for freely sharing her knowledge of publishing.

Most of all, I give thanks to my friends at *AM Northwest* and *Town Hall*, especially Janice Bangs, Chris Harrison, Carolyn Stanton, Kerri Williamson, and Lauren Moughon, for their constant encouragement, creative suggestions, and moral support; to my wife, Kari, for her labors bringing our wonderful son, David, into this world; to David, for all he teaches me each day; to Paul, brother in my family of choice, for always being there; and to my mother, Gretta, whose memory inspires me still.

amniocentesis. A test usually carried out in second trimester to look for fetal defects or fetal maturity. Done by extracting amniotic fluid through mom's abdomen by needle.

amniotic fluid. The fluid surrounding the fetus in the uterus.

analgesics. Drugs often used during labor that manage pain while allowing mom to remain conscious.

anesthetic, general. A painkiller that causes loss of feeling in the entire body, leaving mom unconscious.

anesthetic, regional or local. A painkiller that causes loss of feeling in a specific part of mom's body. See *spinal, caudal, epidural.*

Apgar scale, score, or test. A test performed immediately at birth to assess the newborn's physical condition. Scored from a low of 0 to a high of 10, the test evaluates heart rate, respiratory effort, muscle tone, reflexes, and skin color. An ideal score is between 7 and 10.

Bradley method. A birthing approach that trains dad to distract his partner from pain by redirecting her focus toward different parts of her body.

Braxton Hicks contractions. Irregular contractions of the uterus, especially later in pregnancy. Often mistaken for the start of labor and called "false labor."

breech. The position of a baby that is upside down (bottom down) in the uterus.

caudal. A local anesthetic injected into the base of the spine to ease pain during labor and delivery.

cervix. The neck-shaped lower entrance to the uterus.

Cesarean section. Delivery of the baby through a cut in the abdominal and uterine walls. Usually done to protect the health of mother or child.

colostrum. A yellowish fluid rich in minerals that the baby needs. It is secreted by the breasts late in pregnancy and for the first few days after birth before mom's milk comes in.

contractions. The regular tightening of the muscles in the uterus as they work to open the cervix in labor and then push the baby down the birth canal.

couvade syndrome. Symptoms associated with pregnancy that are experienced by the father-to-be.

dilation. The gradual opening of the cervix caused by contractions of the uterus during labor.

effacement. The gradual shortening of the cervical canal in the final month of pregnancy and into the first stage of labor. A measure of the progression of labor.

embryo. The fertilized egg in the uterus from conception through the first eight weeks of development. Thereafter, the fetus.

engorgement. The overfilling of the breasts with milk.

epidural. A local anesthetic injected through a catheter into the epidural space in the lower spine to ease pain during labor and delivery.

episiotomy. A surgical cut made to enlarge the vagina to ease delivery.

fetus. The unborn baby in the uterus from the eighth week until birth.

gestation. The time between conception and delivery.

gynecologist. A doctor specializing in female medicine.

hypertension. High blood pressure that, in pregnancy, can be associated with many problems, including reduced blood flow to the fetus.

induced labor, or induction. The process of artificially starting labor and keeping it going.

jaundice. A yellowing of the skin of the newborn that occurs in about half of all births. Jaundice is caused by immaturity of the newborn's liver and is usually easily treated with bright light.

kegels. Exercises that strengthen the pelvic-floor muscles.

lactation. The production of milk by the breasts.

Lamaze method. A birthing method based on coached relaxation and breathing techniques that are synchronized to the expectant mother's contractions.

LeBoyer method. A birthing method designed to create peaceful entry into the world for the baby: low lighting, immediate holding of baby by mom, and a calm delivery-room atmosphere.

meconium. The dark green or black fecal matter present in the baby's bowel before birth and passed in the first few days after delivery.

oxytocin. A natural hormone that stimulates uterine contractions and the glands that produce breast milk.

perinatal. The period from the twenty-eighth week of pregnancy to one week after birth.

perineum. The area surrounding the vagina and between the vagina and the rectum. Delivery can tear the perineum or leave it swollen and tender.

Pitocin. A synthetic form of the hormone oxytocin. Pitocin is used to artificially induce or speed along labor.

placenta. The organ that develops on the lining of the uterus and supplies the fetus with nutrients. After birth of the child, the placenta is also delivered from the uterus.

postpartum. After delivery.

prenatal. Before delivery.

psychoprophylaxis. Another term for the Lamaze method of childbirth based on breathing techniques.

pudendal. A local anesthetic injection to numb the nerves in the perineum.

show, or bloody show. A bloody or pink vaginal discharge a few days or hours before labor begins. A sign that labor is starting.

spinal. A local anesthetic injected into the spinal cord to ease pain during labor and delivery.

ultrasound. A diagnostic test used to assess baby's development and health (and sex!). A device that creates an image of the fetus from reflected high-frequency sound waves.

uterus. The hollow, muscular organ in the pelvic cavity where the fertilized egg implants and develops into the fetus.

BIBLIOGRAPHY AND RESOURCES

Just in case reading this book has inspired you to match your partner's zeal in learning everything there is to know about pregnancy, I have compiled a list of the sources used in this book as well as additional resources that have proved helpful to other expectant parents. This is by no means a complete list of all that has been said about pregnancy, but it should be more than enough to keep you and your partner busy through several pregnancies.

Books

Atalla, Bill M., and Stephen Beitler. *The Thirteen Months of Pregnancy: A Guide for the Pregnant Father.* Kenwood, Calif.: Oddly Enough Press, 1992.

Ash, Jennifer, and Armin A. Brott. *Expectant Fathers: Facts, Tips, and Advice for Dads-to-Be.* New York: Abbeville Press, 1995.

Eisenberg, Arlene, Heidi Murkoff, and Sandee Hathaway. *What to Expect When You're Expecting.* New York: Workman, 1992.

Evans, Cleveland Kent. *Unusual and Most Popular Baby Names.* Lincolnwood, Ill.: Publications International Ltd., 1996.

Evans, Nancy. *The A-to-Z of Pregnancy and Childbirth: A Concise Encyclopedia.* Alameda, Calif.: Hunter House, 1994.

Heinowitz, Jack. *Pregnant Fathers: Challenges and Discoveries on the Road to Being a Father.* Kansas City, Mo.: Andrews & McMeel, 1997.

Iovine, Vicki. *The Girlfriends' Guide to Pregnancy Daily Diary*. New York: Pocket Books, 1995.

Kitzinger, Sheila. *The Complete Book of Pregnancy and Childbirth*. New York: Knopf, 1996.

Lauersen, Niels, and Judy Hendra. *It's Your Pregnancy: Questions You Ask Yourself and Are Afraid to Ask Your Obstetrician*. New York: Fireside, 1987.

Marshall, Connie. *The Expectant Father: Helping the Father-to-Be Understand and Become Part of the Pregnancy Experience*. Rocklin, Calif.: Prima Publishing, 1992.

Rothman, Barbara Katz, ed. *Encyclopedia of Childbearing*. New York: Holt, 1993.

Shapiro, Jerrold Lee. *When Men Are Pregnant: Needs and Concerns of Expectant Fathers*. New York: Dell Publishing, 1993.

Simpkin, Penny. *The Birth Partner: Everything You Need to Know to Help a Woman through Childbirth*. Boston: Harvard Common Press, 1989.

Articles

Locker, Hillary. "How Men Can Get Involved." *American Baby*, November 1994.

Pennebaker, Ruth. "I'm Going to Be a Dad." *Parents*, November 1994.

Pennebaker, Ruth. "The Perfect Pregnant Father." *Parents*, August 1994.

Shannon, Jacqueline. "Pregnancy Pounds: What You Gain Helps Guarantee a Healthy Baby." *Parents*, March 1997.

Stevenson-Smith, Fay. "Dads in the Labor Room." *Parents*, January 1993.

————. "Mother's Helper." *American Baby*, August 1996.

Web sources

http://www.parenthoodweb.com

Other sources

American College of Obstetricians and Gynecologists
409 12th Street, S.W.
Washington, D.C. 20004
202-638-5577

The American College of Nurse Midwives
818 Connecticut Ave., N.W., Suite 900
Washington, D.C. 20006
202-728-9874